Screen Shots

Real-time communication

on the Internet

Real-time communication on the Internet

Jean-Paul
Mesters

CASSELL&CO

First published, revised and adapted, in the United Kingdom in 2000 by Hachette UK

© English Translation Hachette UK 2000
© Hachette Livre: Marabout Informatique 1998

English translation by Prose Unlimited
Concept and editorial direction: Ghéorghïi Vladimirovitch Grigorieff
Additional research and editorial assistance: Peter Murray, Simon Woolf, Martin Davies, Jane Eady, Marylin Grant, Johan Rinchard and John Cardinal.

A CIP catalogue for this book is available from the British Library

Trademarks/Registered Trademarks

Computer hardware and software brand names mentioned in this book are protected by their respective trademarks and acknowledged. Every effort has been made to make this book as complete and accurate as possible, but the publisher and author cannot accept any responsibility for any loss or inconvenience sustained by any reader as a result of this book's information or advice.

ISBN 1 84202 040 4

Designed by Graph'M
Layout by Jean-Paul Mesters
Typeset in Humanist 521
Printed and bound by Graficas Estella, Spain

Hachette UK
Cassell & Co
The Orion Publishing Group
Wellington House
London
WC2R 0BB

Web site: www.marabout.com/Cassell

Contents

How to use this book

Welcome to this visual guide. It explains how to carry out some one hundred or so operations, ranging from the simple to the more complex, in a clear and methodical manner.

The book is divided into thematic chapters, which are in turn divided into sections. Each section deals with a separate topic and explains its many facets and uses, as well as detailing all related commands.

The orange 'Checklist' bookmarks that appear throughout the book contain lists of the procedures you must follow in order to complete a given task successfully. The accompanying screen shots have arrows pointing to certain parts of the screen. When the points in the Checklists are numbered, they correspond directly with these numbered green arrows. When the points in the bookmarks bear letters they do not relate directly to the arrows, but simply provide additional useful information. When the arrows pointing to the screen are orange they give information on a particular feature, whilst the red arrows alert you of a possible danger, such as a button to avoid pressing at all costs!

In addition to illustrations of relevant screen shots as they should appear if instructions have been followed correctly, the Screen Shots series also features 'Tips' boxes and 'light-bulb' features that will help you get the most out of the programs. Shortcut keys are useful ways of saving time for frequently used commands. The 'Tips' boxes give these handy time-saving hints, while the light-bulb features provide additional information by presenting an associated command, option or a particular type of use for the command. Finally, to reassure you that you are on the right path, flow charts summarising the screens through which you have just worked, appear at intervals throughout the book.

Happy reading

Introduction

The Internet has many fantastic features: email, the World Wide Web, Newsgroups, FTP servers, but it also opens up enormous possibilities for communication in real time. This means that you can be in live, direct contact on the Net with another user, who could be in the next house, the next town or even in the next country. With real-time communication you can chat to a friend via the Net as easily as if you were chatting over a cup of coffee in a café. There are many software applications for this method of communication, ranging from simple programs for sending and receiving short messages to sophisticated, video-conferencing software. It would be impossible to include all of them in this book. Consequently, we cover a few of the most popular ones for both the Windows and Macintosh environments.

This book is divided into two main parts. Part I deals with the oldest communication system: the IRC. The IRC network is still widely used by both professionals and amateurs, including surfers in search of cyber companionship and a few hours of casual chatting. Part II deals with direct communication software that enables you to stay in touch with your friends and relations, to know who is on line, and to chat directly to them. These systems reflect the enormous scope that the Internet provides for instant and efficient communication. For newcomers, the appendix defines the technical terms and jargon used in the world of Internet communications. You can thus dive straight into the IRC channels, without having to ask what 'lol' or <g> means. A small table lists the most frequently used smileys.
Have fun !

You can contact the author on:
jip@soleil.org
3259825@pager.mirabilis.com
UIN - ICQ# : 3259825

Part 1: Introduction

IRC

Some web portals featuring a chat area

Some sites feature chat rooms. You don't need any special software to use them: a simple browser will do. Just choose the topic you are interested in, enter the chat room and join the chat in progress.

 **Yahoo! Chat (http://uk.chat.yahoo.com):** many different topics including art, computers, games, hobbies, music, family, religion, health and so on (see page 23).

 **Talk City (http://talkcity.com):** wide range of chat topics. Talk City also features a calendar of events in the different chat rooms and informs surfers when celebrities drop in.

 **Warner Bros Chat Complex (http://chat.warnerbros.com):** discussions on Warner Bros productions (television, cinema and music).

 **Sports WebBoard (http://www.sportswebboard.com):** baseball, basketball, football, soccer and so on.

 **Ultimate Chatlist (http://www.chatlist.com):** a list of chat rooms by topics with search by keywords.

What is IRC ?

IRC resembles a huge building. When you push open the front door, you find yourself in a hall with thousands of doors. Behind each door is a chat room which may be empty or occupied by a number of people chatting. Each door bears a label with the name of the room. Enter the room of your choice. The list of occupants is displayed and you can take part in the chat immediately. In more technical terms, IRC (Internet Relay Chat) is a multi-user, real-time communication system where you can chat on line with other people in channels (i.e. chat rooms devoted to specific topics).

IRC is an integrated part of the Internet while remaining operationally independent. It uses the Internet for the physical transmission of messages, but has its own servers (i.e. the computers used to transmit the messages). When your computer is connected to IRC (with an ad hoc program), it becomes a client of one of the servers.

There are several IRC networks operating throughout the world, each being independent of the others. Four such IRCs are active in Europe. They are called **IRCnet**, **Efnet**, **UnderNet** and **DalNet**. Each network is completely separate: its servers and the channels it offers are never shared with the other networks. In practical terms, when you connect to a server, you enter a very specific IRC network and have access only to the channels available in this network.

You do not have to use specialised software to chat and communicate on the Internet. Some websites and many Web portals feature a chat area that can be accessed free with any browser. All you have to do to join a chat is to register. See page 23 for information on the Yahoo! chat page. Also try the Dobedo chatsite (http://www.dobedo.co.uk).

IRC network servers

If you cannot wait to dive into **IRC**, then skip directly to the chapter on the software you are using. If you do not know which software you are using, see the list of the most popular programs at the end of this chapter.

You must indicate the name of the server to which you connect in your **IRC** software . Here are a few **European** servers for the four main networks.

DalNet

defiant.uk.eu.DAL.net (United Kingdom)
ced.se.eu.DAL.net (Sweden)
arlington.va.us.DAL.net (Norway)
A complete list of servers is given at the following address: **http://www.dal.net**

UnderNet

london.UK.EU.undernet.org (London)
caen.FR.EU.Undernet.Org (Caen - France)
antwerpen.BE.EU.undernet.org (Antwerp - Belgium)
diemen.NL.EU.undernet.org (Netherlands)
goettingen.DE.EU.undernet.org (Göttingen - Germany)
A complete list of servers is given at the following address:
http://servers.undernet.org

You will find a complete list of IRC network servers at the following address: **http://www.irchelp. org/irchelp/networks /servers**

EFNet (Eris Free Net)

efnet.demon.co.uk (United Kingdom)
irc.magic.ca (Canada)
irc.stanford.edu (United States)
A complete list of servers is given at the following address:
http://www.irchelp.org/irchelp/networks/servers/efnet.html

IRCNet

eris.bt.net (London)
irc.netcom.net.uk (London)
irc.u-net.com (Cheshire - United Kingdom)
irc.easynet.co.uk (London)
irc.belnet.be (Brussels)
ircnet.online.be (Brussels)
irc.vub.ac.be (Brussels)
irc.skybel.net (Brussels)
irc.emn.fr (Nantes - France)
irc.enst.fr (Paris)
salambo.enserb.u-bordeaux.fr (Bordeaux - France)
irc.grolier.net (Paris)
irc.fu-berlin.de (Berlin)
irc.netsurf.de (Hamburg)
irc.rz.uni-karlsruhe.de (Karlsruhe - Germany)
irc.sci.kun.nl (Nijmegen - Netherlands)
irc2.sci.kun.nl (Nijmegen - Netherlands)
irc.xs4all.nl (Amsterdam)
irc.datacomm.ch (Basle - Switzerland)
A complete list of servers is given at the following address:
http://www.irchelp.org/irchelp/networks/servers/ircnet.html

IRC commands

These commands are recognised by most **IRC** servers. You enter them at the keyboard where you type the messages you send. They are all preceded by the / sign. This sign is indispensable: without it, all the users of the channel would receive the text of your commands!

Using the channel

/away message	You leave your keyboard briefly. The message will be sent to those who try to contact you directly, with /msg for example. When you are operational again, use the command /away with no following text.
	/away I'll get a cup of coffee and be right back
/ctcp nickname finger	Provides the e-mail address of the indicated user.
	/ctcp phil finger
/ctcp nickname ping	Sends a ping to the user mentioned (to find out his or her computer's response time).
	/ctcp phil ping
/ctcp nickname version	Displays the name of the IRC software of the indicated user.
	/ctcp phil version
/dcc chat nickname	Asks for a private (DCC) chat with the user mentioned. The connection will no longer go via the IRC server. It will be direct.
	/dcc chat phil
/dcc get nickname	Accepts a file sent to you by the user indicated.
	/dcc get phil
/dcc send nickname filename	Sends a file to the user mentioned. Indicate the access path to the file.
	/dcc send phil bookmarks.htm
/dns nickname	Provides the IP address and the domain name of the user mentioned.
	/dns phil
/ignore nickname	Everything coming from the indicated user will be ignored.
	/ignore phil
/invite nickname	Invites another user to join the channel you are in.
	/invite phil
/me message	Provides information on an action you are carrying out.
	/me I am eating

/msg nickname message	**Sends a private message to the user whose nickname is indicated. To send the message to several users, separate the different recipients by a comma.** /msg joss hello
/msg #channel message	**Sends a public message to all the users of the indicated channel. It is not necessary to be in the channel to send this type of message (the name of the channels is always preceded by the hash mark #).** /msg marabout Ask for our new developments
/notice nickname text	**Sends a note to a specific user. This command is similar to /msg.** /notice phil call me
/notify nickname	**You will be informed when the user mentioned joins the channel.** /notify phil
/part #channel	**You leave the indicated channel.** /part #marabout
/part *	**You leave all the channels.** /part
/query nickname message	**Opens a direct connection window between the indicated user and yourself to transmit private messages. This is equivalent to exchanging private messages with the /msg command. The messages always go through the IRC server.** /query phil hello
/whois nickname	**Displays information on the user mentioned.** /whois joss

The server

/join #channel	**You join the channel indicated. If the channel does not exist, a new one will be created, and you will automatically become the operator.** /join marabout
/join #channel, #channel	**You join the indicated channels.** /join #france+,#france2
/join #channel Password	**If a password exists for joining the channel, enter this password.** /join #CIA secret
/list	**Displays the list of all the channels available.** /list
/list *text*	**Displays the list of channels whose name contains the indicated text.** /list *king*
/list -min x -max x	**Displays the list of channels in which the number of participants is greater than the indicated minimum or lower than the indicated maximum.** /list -min 3 /list -max 10 /list -min 3 -max 10

/map	**Displays the organisation and the address of the Undernet servers.** /map
/names #channel	**Displays the nickname of the users of the indicated channel. If the channel is not mentioned, it displays the list of users of all the channels.** /names #marabout
/nick nickname	**Enables you to change your nickname.** /nick joss fred
/quit	**You quit the channel and the IRC network.** /quit
/quit message	**You quit the channel and the IRC network while sending a message to the users of the channel.** /quit See you tomorrow
/server server	**You connect to the indicated server.** /server eris.bt.net
/time	**Displays the local time of the server to which you are connected.** /time
/who channel	**Displays the nickname and the address of the users connected to the indicated channel. If the channel is not indicated, the command is applied to the current channel.** /who #marabout
/stats d	**Displays the statistics of the server on the data indicated by d:**

b	**for the banned users**	*c*	**for the connections**
i	**for the domain names**	*k*	**for the users**
m	**for the server commands**	*u*	**the time since the last re-initialisation of the server**

/stats c

For operators only

/mode #channel mode	**Changes a mode of the indicated channel. See the modes below.** /mode #marabout n
/mode #channelmode nickname	**Changes a mode for the indicated user. See the modes below.** /mode #marabout l phil
/kick nickname	**Kicks the indicated user out of the channel (see glossary).** /kick phil
/topic text	**Defines the text indicated as the topic of the channel.** /topic Welcome

IRC modes

'User' modes

o   The operator status is attributed to (+o) or removed from (-o) a user.

i   Makes the user invisible during the /who and /names commands. The user remains visible in the list of channel users. It is the only /mode command available to the standard user. It is impossible to make another user invisible.

b   The user is banned (+b). S/he cannot join the channel.

s   The user can receive messages from the server.

v   Gives the floor to a user in a moderated channel.

'Channel' modes

t   Fixes the topic. Users will not be able to change this topic.

i   Access to the channel by invitation.

p   Private channel. In the channels list, the name of the channel is replaced by **Prv**. When you enter the /whois command, it does not appear in the list of channels to which you are connected. To join this channel you must know its real name.

s   Secret channel. Its name does not appear at all after the /list command. The p and s modes are exclusive. To join this channel, you must know its real name.

m   Moderated channel. Anyone can join, but only the operators and users in the v mode have the right to talk.

n   Blocks the entry of notices and messages from outside.

l (x)   Limits the channel to x number of users at the most.

k   A password is required to join the channel.

Examples		
	/mode #channel	Displays the modes of the channel.
	/mode #marabout k vulcan	The password 'vulcan' is required if you wish to join the channel.
	/mode #marabout o phil	**Phil is opped** : he obtains operator status.
	/mode #marabout -o phil	**Phil is de-opped.**
	/mode phil i	**Phil opts for invisibility for himself.**

If you do not wish to be disturbed in a channel where you are the operator, attribute to this channel the +i, +s, +n, +k and +t modes.

An IRC session

Connecting

Start by connecting to a server. Bear in mind that there are four independent networks in Europe and that they do not offer the same channels. Connect to the server nearest you to reduce the response time and limit the load to a minimum. See the list of servers on page 12.

A glossary at the end of this book will help you understand the vocabulary and jargon used in the world of communications.

TIP

IRC is a public network. Everybody can connect to it, so be careful and do not trust strangers. A nickname is not the property of a given user: anyone may use it. You can always verify the identity of someone with the /whois command. Do not give too much personal information in the configuration settings of the connection, and in particular do not give your personal address, telephone number or real name.

A server refuses your request to connect. Why?
It is out of order.
It is overloaded.
Your nickname is already used by someone else.
Your Internet domain is refused by the server (e.g. because some users of this domain have violated IRC etiquette).
Your Internet domain is not provided by the server.

In all these cases, the fastest solution is to try another server (or to change nickname if that is the problem).

If you are hoping to join a specific channel, you must know the network in which it is offered. If you make an appointment with someone, do not forget to specify the network.

You will find the list of English-speaking channels on the different networks at the following address: **http://bishop.mc.duke. edu/irchelp/chanlist**

Which channel do you wish to join?
If you are a regular, there is no need to search around: you join your favourite channel immediately. But if you are searching for a channel, you must start by displaying a list of all the channels available. The names of the channels always start with the # symbol (for a global channel accessible in the entire network, irrespective of the server) or by & (for a local channel, accessible only by users connected to the server on which it was created). This list is very extensive. There are more than 6,000 channels on IRCNet and more than 10,000 on UnderNet! Fortunately, the IRC software enables you to filter the channels accordingly and to save the list of your favourites.

The IRC servers make no distinction between upper and lower case. The channel #Diamond is therefore the same as #DIAMOND or #diamond.

You cannot join a channel. Why?
You are banned from the channel. An operator bars access to you or the Internet domain to which you belong.
The maximum number of participants (determined by the channel operators) has been reached.
The channel can be joined by invitation only.
A password is required.

Talk now

Rules of good conduct

Use the current language in the channel.

Say hello (hi) when you join the channel but avoid greeting every newcomer (as this causes unnecessary overload).

Avoid insults, rude jokes, or racist and offensive remarks. Not only is it not nice but you never know who is hiding behind a nickname.

Do not write in upper case (it's like shouting).

Some servers do not recognise accented characters. Look at the messages exchanged to check whether accents are used.

When you join a channel you do not know, observe the exchanges for some time before taking part in the discussion. You can thus decide whether the subject and the tone of the chat are right for you.

Do not get angry if no one replies to your messages. The transmission times may be long; or your messages may remain invisible if the other users have put you on their ban list.

Do not flood the channel with too many lines at a time; you might be kicked out.

These are unwritten rules which, nevertheless, it is good practice to obey.

Notes

Most of the messages are public, and are received by all the participants in the channel.

Others are private and are received only by the recipient you indicate.

You can also establish a direct connection (outside the IRC network) with a user of your choice (DCC) for a private (DCC) chat or to send files.

Channel Operator

When you create a channel you become the operator (or boss) of that channel. You can then change the status and operator of the channel (the modes).

You can also kick out or ban a user (exclude him or her temporarily or permanently).

Your channel will exist as long as you maintain it. In other words, as soon as the last participant leaves, the channel disappears. All its parameters and its ban list will also disappear.

IRC software

mIRC

This is one of the oldest and best known pieces of chat software. It runs only on **PC** and comes in two versions: a 16-bit version for Windows 3.x and a 32-bit version for Windows 95, 98, 2000 and **NT4**. It is a complete program in terms of commands and configuration alike. Most commands are contained in the menus, which saves you from having to enter them yourself on the keyboard: a simple click does the trick. See page 27.

IRCle

This is the most famous **IRC** software in the Macintosh world. As well known as mIRC, it has virtually the same features. Its major advantage is that it fits perfectly in the Macintosh environment, and is therefore very comfortable to use. See page 61.

Visual IRC

Visual **IRC** is probably one of the fastest and most complete software available at this time. It comes with several automatic scripts and the **ViRCScript** language so that you can program scripts yourself. Moreover, it is equipped with audio and video communications and to share a drawing screen. Its menu system can be entirely personalised and its window system is fully compatible with Windows 95, 98, 2000 and **NT**. Try it!

Publisher: MeGALiTH
Publisher's website: http://www.megalith.co.uk
Freeware
System requirements: Windows 95, 98, NT4, 2000
Download from: http://www.megalith.co.uk/index_download.html

Microsoft Chat

Supplied by Microsoft with Internet Explorer 4 and 5 or with Windows 98, it is the most entertaining chat software for the **PC**. Although not as advanced as mIRC, it is more user-friendly and features all the essential commands and functions. Its originality lies in its 'comic strip' interface. Each participant chooses his or her character (the expressions of which are modifiable) and the landscape in which the chat is to take place. This should not stop you from chatting in the conventional 'text' mode, however.

Publisher: Microsoft
Publisher's website: http://www.microsoft.com/catalog
Freeware
System requirements: Windows 95, 98, NT4, 2000 (Internet Explorer is not essential).
Download from: http://mschus.www.conxion.com/msdownload/mschat/2.5/x86/en/MSCHAT25.EXE

A complement to any version of Microsoft Chat, the Microsoft Chat Software Development Kit, which you can use to integrate Microsoft Chat in a webpage of your site, can be obtained from:
http://msdn.microsoft.com/developer/sdk/chatsdk/chatcontrol.asp (1 Mb)

PIRCH

This is the most sophisticated **IRC** software. It features simultaneous connection to several servers, the transmission of video images, and automatic redialling, and accepts without difficulty the integration of multimedia software such as **Real Player**.

Publisher: Northwest Computer Services
Publisher's website: http://www.pirchat.com
Freeware
System requirements: Windows 95, 98, NT4, 2000
Download from: http://www.pirchat.com/download.html

Checklist

1. Use your browser to connect to the Yahoo! site at **http://uk.chat.yahoo.com**

2. If you have not yet signed up, click Sign Up for Yahoo! Chat to do so.

3. If you have already signed up, enter your Yahoo! ID.

4. Enter your password.

5. Click the Sign in button.

The first time you access the chat page, a security message will ask you if you want to install and run Yahoo! Chat. Click Yes.

The Yahoo! portal site

YAHOO! Chat

Click here to sign up in the Yahoo! Community.

Don't have a Yahoo! ID?

Sign Up For Yahoo! Chat!
thousands of people, hundreds of chat rooms, nothing to download!

Enter your Yahoo! ID

You are not currently signed in.

Yahoo! ID: [ ]

Password: [ ]   [Sign in]

☐ Remember my ID & Password (What's this?)

Enter your password.

Click this button to sign in.

Click here if you don't remember your password.

Click a link to access one of the chat rooms.

Click this button to select your favourite chat rooms: they will be displayed here so you can access them rapidly.

YAHOO! Chat   Home - Yahoo! - Acct Info - Sign Out

Welcome, jip511 ▾ [add / change profile]   Chat Software: Java ▾

Yahoo! Chat   Events Calendar - Transcripts - Help

| Main | Movies, TV | Music | News, Finance, Sports | Health, Family | Teen |

Announcements
- NEW! **Voice Chat** - Try out our new **voice chat!** For more info, see our **help section**.
- We're looking for **Chat Engineers**.
- **Alloy Contest:** **Brian McBride**

Upcoming Events

Featured Rooms
- Chat Central - Chat Central, jump in and start talking.
- Traveler's Room - Looking for a good place to go? Ask someone in the Travel room.
- Trivia Madness! - Do trivial factoids fill your brain? Match wits with other Trivia masters.

Favorite Rooms   [Edit]

You have not yet selected any favorite rooms.

Click the **Edit** button to add rooms to this list.

Friends in Chat   [Edit]

Select a friend and click the "Go to Friend" button to join them in chat.

[- no friends online -]   [Go to Friend]

Chat

Notes

Web portals have their own chat server. The chat rooms made available are not public: they are accessible only by their server on their website.

Not all IRC commands are recognised by these private servers, but the rules of good conduct (Netiquette) still apply.

Messages from the system

Messages sent by the participants

Name of the chat room

List of chat room participants.

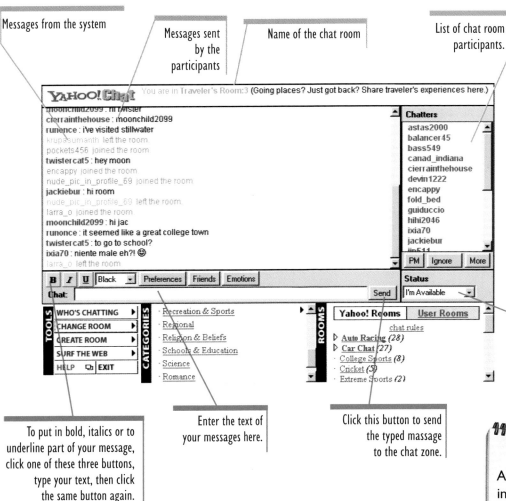

To put in bold, italics or to underline part of your message, click one of these three buttons, type your text, then click the same button again.

Enter the text of your messages here.

Click this button to send the typed massage to the chat zone.

Click here to select your status, and so let the other participants know whether you are at your computer.

All participants in the chat room will see the messages you sent.

Notes

To find out the status of a participant, point to his or her name with the mouse without clicking.

The private message window is displayed when you send or receive a private message.

The nickname of an active participant is displayed in bold.

PM, Ignore and More buttons

Click this button to open the send private message window to the selected participant.

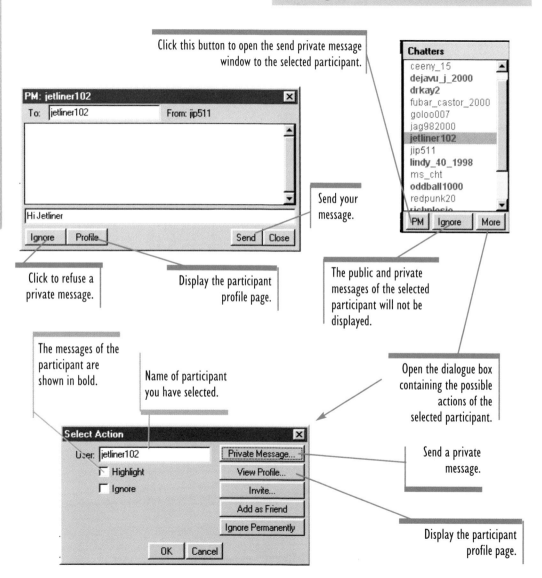

PM: jetliner102

To: jetliner102   From: jip511

Hi Jetliner

Ignore   Profile   Send   Close

Click to refuse a private message.

Display the participant profile page.

Chatters
ceeny_15
dejavu_j_2000
drkay2
fubar_castor_2000
goloo007
jag982000
jetliner102
jip511
lindy_40_1998
ms_cht
oddball1000
redpunk20

PM   Ignore   More

Send your message.

The public and private messages of the selected participant will not be displayed.

Hint
To send a private message, double click the participant's name

The messages of the participant are shown in bold.

Name of participant you have selected.

Open the dialogue box containing the possible actions of the selected participant.

Select Action

User: jetliner102

☐ Highlight
☐ Ignore

Private Message...
View Profile...
Invite...
Add as Friend
Ignore Permanently

OK   Cancel

Send a private message.

Display the participant profile page.

Chat rooms

CHANGE ROOM buttons

Click this button.

Click a category.

Click the name of the chat room you want.

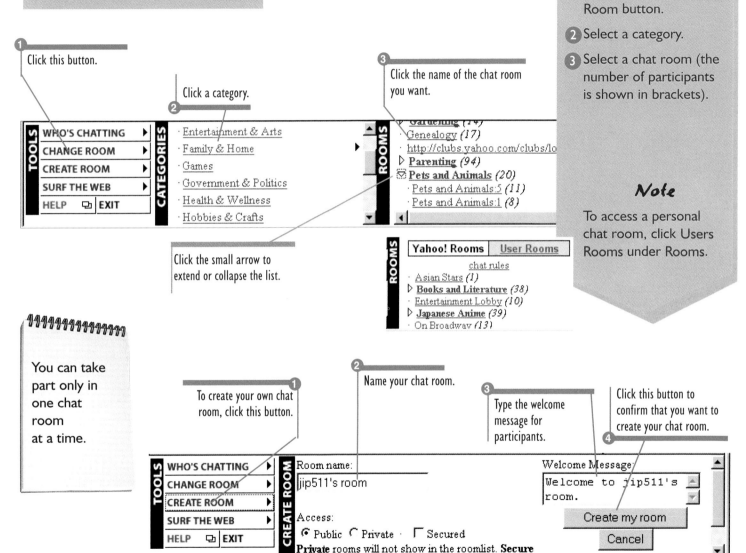

Click the small arrow to extend or collapse the list.

You can take part only in one chat room at a time.

To create your own chat room, click this button.

Name your chat room.

Type the welcome message for participants.

Click this button to confirm that you want to create your chat room.

Checklist

1. To choose another chat room, click the Change Room button.

2. Select a category.

3. Select a chat room (the number of participants is shown in brackets).

Note

To access a personal chat room, click Users Rooms under Rooms.

Chapter 1

mIRC

Introducing mIRC

This is the oldest software for IRC connections.
Publisher's website: http://www.mirc.co.uk
Shareware
**System requirements: Windows 95, 98, NT4, 2000 (for the 32-bit version) and
Windows 3.x (for the 16-bit version)**
Download from the publisher's site:
mIRC 16 bits (952 Kb) or mIRC 32 bits (1 Mb): http://www.mirc.co.uk/get.html

TIP

What can you do with mIRC?

Establish a connection with a server from any IRC network.

Consult and filter a list of channels.

Send and receive private and public messages.

Ignore unwelcome users.

Obtain information on the users of a channel.

Establish a DCC connection for a private (DCC) chat or in order to send files.

Create and have full control over your own channel.

Connect

Start/Programs/mIRC

When you connect for the first time you must provide the following information: the name of the server to which you connect, your nickname, name and your e-mail address. These details remain valid for all future connections, but nothing prevents you from changing them. Your nickname is not definitive because you can change it whenever you want without having to disconnect. Once you have connected to the server, you can join virtually all the channels and start to chat immediately.

When the installation has been completed, you can open mIRC from the **Start** menu. Click on the **Start** button, then on **Programs**. Click on the **mIRC** folder and then on the **mIRC32** command.

HOW TO
At **http://www.thezone.pair. com/mirc**
you will find additional help on how to install, set and use the mIRC as well as on the IRC network and the installation of bots.

TIP

Disable the option in the lower left-hand corner of the first dialogue box to prevent it from opening next time you start mIRC.

Checklist

1. Select the File/Options command and click on Connect.

2. Enter your name.

3. Enter your e-mail address.

4. Enter your nickname (9 characters maximum).

5. Enter a back-up nickname just in case the first is no longer available.

6. Select a server from the list.

7. Connect.

Disconnect from the server with the File/Cancel Connect command.

Connecting to a server

2 Enter your name.

3 Enter your e-mail address.

4 Enter your nickname.

These four buttons open the servers list. See page 32.

6 Select a server from the list.

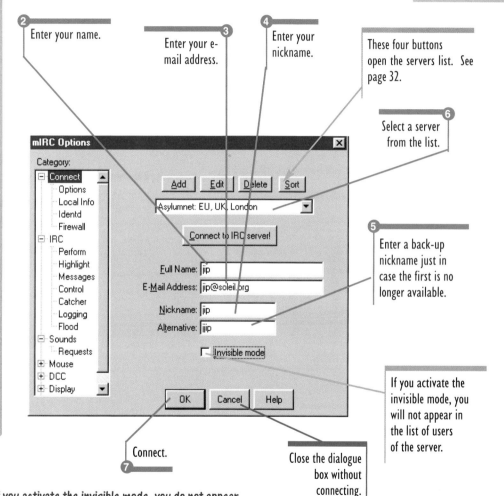

5 Enter a back-up nickname just in case the first is no longer available.

If you activate the invisible mode, you will not appear in the list of users of the server.

7 Connect.

Close the dialogue box without connecting.

If you activate the invisible mode, you do not appear in the list of users of the server, but you will be visible when you join a channel and you could be reached by those who know your nickname.

Alt + o

CHAPTER 1 : MIRC

31

✎ Managing the servers list

File/Options

Description of the server as it appears in the list.

Address of the server.

TCP/IP port number through which the server will transmit the messages. In general, you can leave 6667.

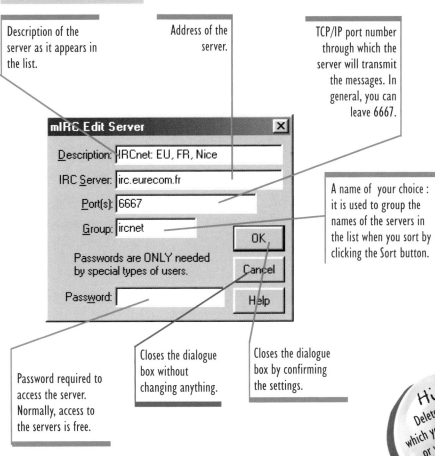

mIRC Edit Server

Description: IRCnet: EU, FR, Nice

IRC Server: irc.eurecom.fr

Port(s): 6667

Group: ircnet

Passwords are ONLY needed by special types of users.

Password:

OK
Cancel
Help

A name of your choice : it is used to group the names of the servers in the list when you sort by clicking the Sort button.

Password required to access the server. Normally, access to the servers is free.

Closes the dialogue box without changing anything.

Closes the dialogue box by confirming the settings.

Hint
Delete servers which you will not use or which are not relevant.

Note

If the server rejects the connection, it displays the message 'Disconnected'.

Name of server.

Your connection time (here I hour).

Your nickname.

Name of computer housing the IRC server and server software version.

Number of users connected to the network.

Number of server operators (IRCop) connected.

Number of chat channels accessible on the network.

Channel modes available on the server (see page 19).

Number of servers in the network.

User's modes available on the server (see page 17).

Number of clients (i.e. computers like yours) connected to the server.

Command entry field.

```
Status: jip [+ir] on irc.enst.fr (01:00)                          _ □ ×
*** Connecting to irc.enst.fr (6667)
-
PING? PONG!
-
Welcome to the Internet Relay Network jip!+jip@18-25.CampusNet.ucl.ac.be
Your host is irc.enst.fr, running version 2.9.5+Cr15+Fl4
This server was created Fri Jun 19 1998 at 22:08:16 MET DST
irc.enst.fr 2.9.5+Cr15+Fl4 oirw abiklmnopqstv
-
There are 24858 users and 7 services on 62 servers
133 operators online
3 unknown connections
10899 channels formed
I have 52 clients, 0 services and 2 servers
-
Message of the Day




End of /MOTD command.
-
Your connection is restricted!
-
*** jip sets mode: +ir
```

Status window

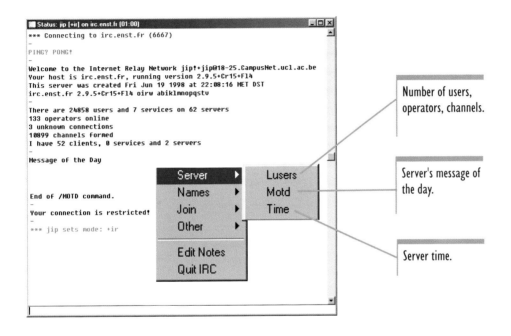

Number of users, operators, channels.

Server's message of the day.

Server time.

To close the **Status** window in the **mIRC** window: select the **Window/Options** command and cancel the **Status** option.

Notes

For more information on the server, click with the right mouse button on the background of the Status window.

The Status window displays throughout the session the result of your commands and the messages sent by the server. Keep an eye on it. Whereas it is independent from the mIRC window, it has its own button in the Windows taskbar. When you click on the mIRC window, it switches to the background. You can restore it to the foreground by clicking on its button in the taskbar.

Join a channel
Commands/Join channel

There are several ways to join a channel. If you know the name of the channel you are interested in, then select the **Commands/Join channel** command. You can also click twice on the name of the channel in the window that lists all the channels. When you have done that, click on the **Join** button in the Channels Folder dialogue box.

You can participate in several channels. A window will open for each channel. You may be denied entry to a channel for several reasons:
- you must be invited by a participant in the channel;
- a password is required;
- you are banned from the channel;
- the maximum number of participants has been reached.

HOW TO

In the Channels List Options dialogue box, you can filter the channels over several character sequences. Separate them by a space. The channels whose names (and where appropriate the descriptions) contain one of the character sequences will be displayed in the list.

TIP

If many windows are open, consider organising them with the Windows/Tile command.

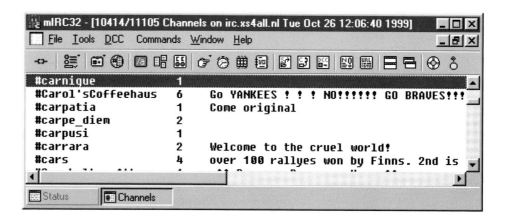

Which channels are available ?

The List Channels button

1 Select and enter the filtering criteria.

2 Lock the exclusion criteria if necessary (a special 'watchful parents' option).

3 Ask the server to provide you with the list or apply the criteria to the list already created by the server.

The channels list is created from the server in the Channels window.

Enter the name of the file in which the channels list will be copied.

The filter options of the dialogue box are applied to the channels list displayed.

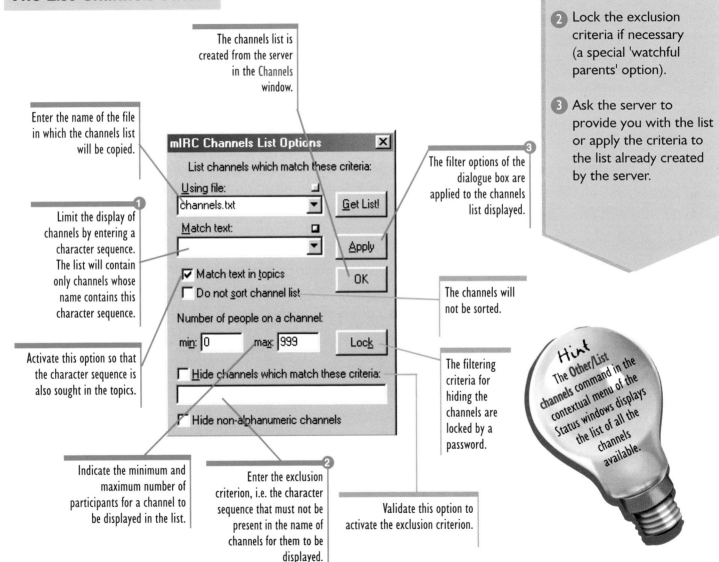

mIRC Channels List Options

List channels which match these criteria:

Using file:
channels.txt   Get List!

Match text:
                                Apply

☑ Match text in topics   OK
☐ Do not sort channel list

Number of people on a channel:

min: 0   max: 999   Lock

☐ Hide channels which match these criteria:

☐ Hide non-alphanumeric channels

Limit the display of channels by entering a character sequence. The list will contain only channels whose name contains this character sequence.

Activate this option so that the character sequence is also sought in the topics.

The channels will not be sorted.

The filtering criteria for hiding the channels are locked by a password.

Indicate the minimum and maximum number of participants for a channel to be displayed in the list.

Enter the exclusion criterion, i.e. the character sequence that must not be present in the name of channels for them to be displayed.

Validate this option to activate the exclusion criterion.

Hint
The Other/List channels command in the contextual menu of the Status windows displays the list of all the channels available.

Other/List channels

Click with the right button in the Status window and select the Other/List channels command.

To open the **Channels List Options** box, select the **Options** command in the contextual menu of the window.

Robots are counted as users. If a channel displays a single user, that user is unlikely to be human.

Number of channels accessible from the server to which you are connected.

Total number of channels in the network.

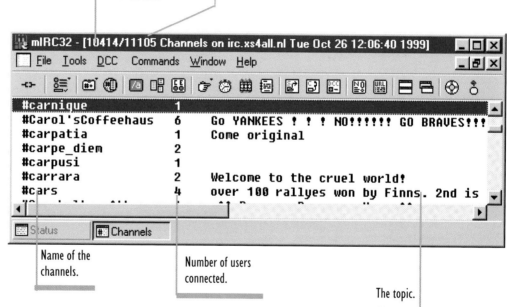

mIRC32 - [10414/11105 Channels on irc.xs4all.nl Tue Oct 26 12:06:40 1999]

File Tools DCC Commands Window Help

```
#carnique            1
#Carol'sCoffeehaus   6    Go YANKEES ! ! ! NO!!!!!! GO BRAVES!!!
#carpatia            1    Come original
#carpe_diem          2
#carpusi             1
#carrara             2    Welcome to the cruel world!
#cars                4    over 100 rallyes won by Finns. 2nd is
```

Status   Channels

Name of the channels.

Number of users connected.

The topic.

Your favourite channels

Channels Folder button

1 In the main windows, click on the Channels Folder button to see the list of your favourite channels (for all networks).

2 Enter the name of the channel to be added to the list.

3 Click on the Add button.

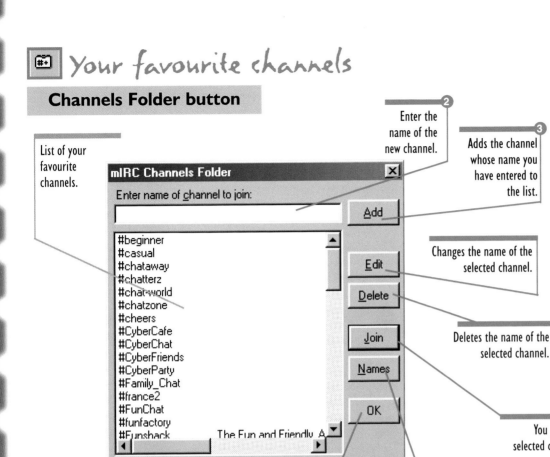

Enter the name of the new channel.

Adds the channel whose name you have entered to the list.

List of your favourite channels.

Changes the name of the selected channel.

Deletes the name of the selected channel.

You join the selected channel.

The list of participants in the selected channel is displayed in the Status window.

If this option is not active, this dialogue box will not open automatically as soon as you have connected to a server.

Closes the dialogue box.

mIRC Channels Folder

Enter name of channel to join:

#beginner
#casual
#chataway
#chatterz
#chat-world
#chatzone
#cheers
#CyberCafe
#CyberChat
#CyberFriends
#CyberParty
#Family_Chat
#france2
#FunChat
#funfactory
#Funshack   The Fun and Friendly A

Add

Edit

Delete

Join

Names

OK

☑ Pop up folder on connect

Add a channel name to the list quickly. Select the channel that interests you from the list. Click on it with the right mouse button and select the Add to folder command.

Checklist

1 In the main window, select the Commands/Join channel command.

2 Enter the name of the channel preceded by a #.

3 You join the channel.

Note

An @ before a nickname indicates that this is a channel operator or a robot.

Commands/Join Channel

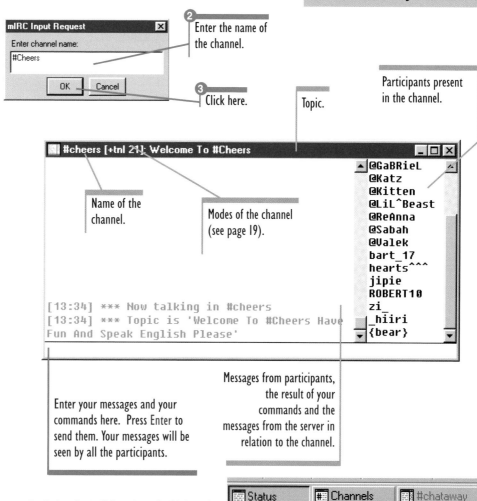

2 Enter the name of the channel.

3 Click here.

Topic.

Participants present in the channel.

Name of the channel.

Modes of the channel (see page 19).

Enter your messages and your commands here. Press Enter to send them. Your messages will be seen by all the participants.

Messages from participants, the result of your commands and the messages from the server in relation to the channel.

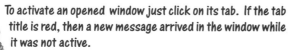

To activate an opened window just click on its tab. If the tab title is red, then a new message arrived in the window while it was not active.

Who is there ?

When you join a channel, the server provides the list of users present (in the Status window). Only the nicknames are displayed.
A nickname does not really provide significant information, but you can obtain more precise details about each user.

Furthermore, if you join a channel frequently, you will get to know other regulars. It is therefore useful to keep their details recorded. This is where the address book comes in.
You can enter a person's e-mail address, site address, some notes, his or her photo and IP address. You can also ask to be informed when a particular user connects to the network.
As this address book is essentially intended for use on the IRC, it is independent of the Outlook, Netscape and Eudora address books.

HOW TO

With the /who command followed by the name of the channel, the server provides some summary information on the users: their nickname, status, logon name and IP address.

H (Here): the user is connected to the IRC network and is active.

G (Gone): the user is connected but not actively involved with his or her session.

*: the user is an IRC operator (IRCop).

@: the user is a channel operator (op).

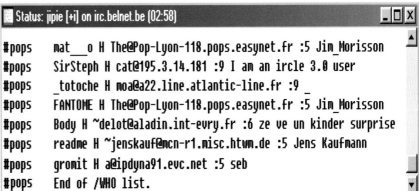

```
Status: jipie [+i] on irc.belnet.be (02:58)                        _ □ X

#pops    mat__o H The@Pop-Lyon-118.pops.easynet.fr :5 Jim_Morisson
#pops    SirSteph H cat@195.3.14.181 :9 I am an ircle 3.0 user
#pops    _totoche H moa@a22.line.atlantic-line.fr :9 _
#pops    FANTOME H The@Pop-Lyon-118.pops.easynet.fr :5 Jim_Morisson
#pops    Body H ~delot@aladin.int-evry.fr :6 ze ve un kinder surprise
#pops    readme H ~jenskauf@mcn-r1.misc.htwm.de :5 Jens Kaufmann
#pops    gromit H a@ipdyna91.evc.net :5 seb
#pops    End of /WHO list.
```

Checklist

1. In the channel window, click on the name of a user with the left button.

2. Now click with the right button and select the UCentral command.

Users identity

UCentral

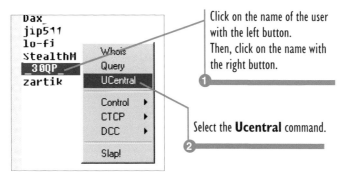

Click on the name of the user with the left button.
Then, click on the name with the right button.

Select the **Ucentral** command.

Name of the channels in which s/he is participating.

Time during which s/he has been idle.

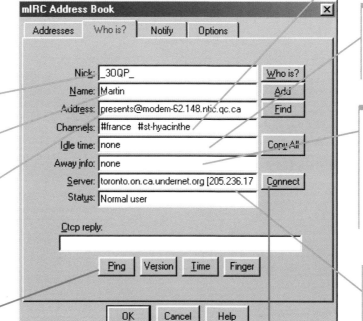

Nickname.

Real (or invented) name.

E-mail address.

If the user is away from the keyboard (with the /away command), the message explaining his/her temporary absence is displayed.

The name of the server to which the user is connected.

Apply one of these commands to the user.

Close the dialogue box.

Connect to the same server as this user.

CHAPTER 1 : MIRC

41

Notes

In the channel window, click with the right button on the selected user and choose the UCentral command.

Click on one of the four buttons.

Ping: the reply time.
Version: the user's software version.
Time: the user's system date and time.
Finger: the user's e-mail.

| Ping | Version | Time | Finger |

Ctcp reply:
2 seconds

Ctcp reply:
Ircle 3.0b10 US PPC 01/08/1998 01:53:57 AM. #9???????

Ctcp reply:
Sat Jan 22 12:32:06 2000

Ctcp reply:
:jip@ping.be :idle 239 second(s)

UCentral

The four commands CTCP **Ping, Version, Time** and **Finger** are available by clicking with the right mouse button on the name of the previously selected user.

/Whois

Name of the host computer (hostname) from which the user is connected.

Name of the user.

Status: jip [+ir] on irc.enst.fr [01:08]

Ariane is A.S@nevers1-232.club-internet.fr * Ariane
Ariane on #millenium #minimal #cookie
Ariane using *.grolier.net IRCNet - Grolier/Clib-Internt
Ariane End of /WHOIS list.

Server to which the user is connected.

Channels in which the user participates.

Notes

Click on the selected user with the right button and select the /whois command.

The result of the command is displayed in the Status window.

Checklist

1. Enter a nickname or select one from the list.

2. Enter the full name.

3. Enter the e-mail address.

4. Enter the new user in the address book or update the details of a user already present.

5. Click OK to save changes.

Hint

To open the address book, enter /uwho in the command and message field.

Address book

Address Book button

Enter a nickname or select it from the list.

Update the address book with the current data.

This button is used to delete a user.

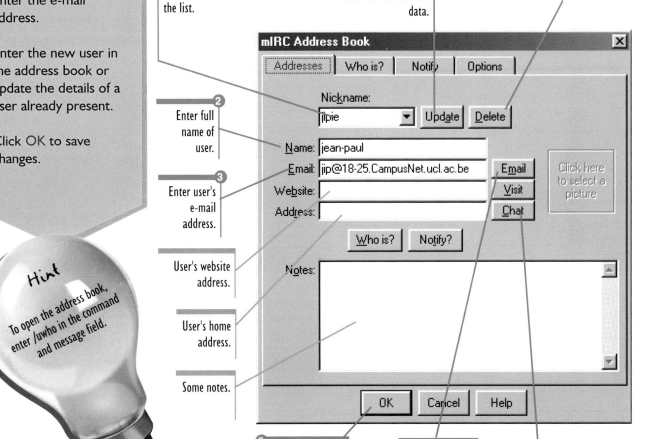

Enter full name of user.

Enter user's e-mail address.

User's website address.

User's home address.

Some notes.

Close the dialogue window and save changes.

Press this button to create an e-mail.

This button sends a private (DCC) chat request.

Address Book flow chart - UCentral

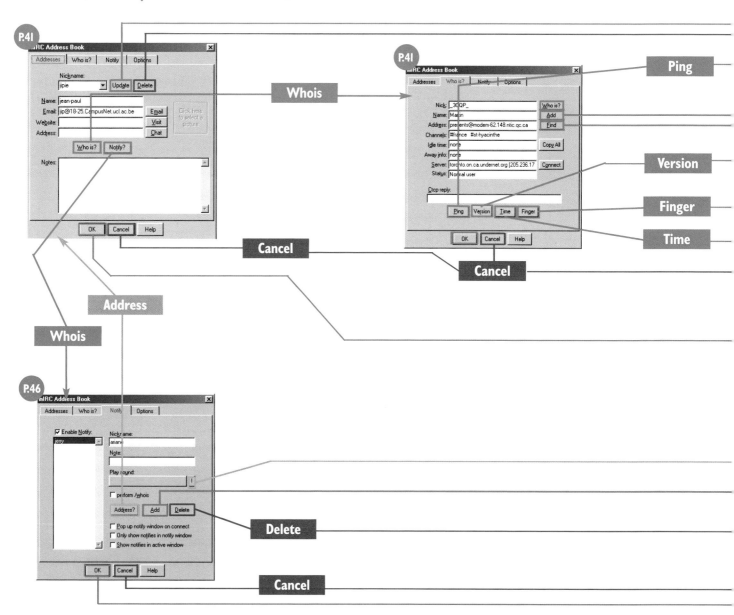

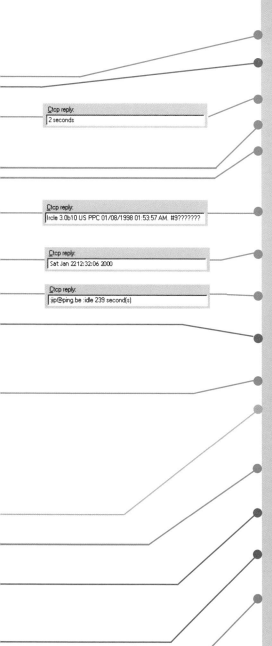

Updates the address book.

Removes user from the address book.

Calculates the ping reception time.

Adds user to the address book.

Searches the address book for the user whose data you have entered.

Returns the user's software name (and version number).

Returns the user's e-mail address.

Returns the user's system date and time.

Closes the dialogue box without saving changes.

Closes the dialogue box and saves changes.

Selects the sound that will be heard when the user connects to the network.

Adds the user to the Notify list.

Deletes user from the Notify list.

Closes the dialogue box without saving the changes.

Closes the dialogue box and saves the parameter values.

Warning

Do not rely on the information provided by the users because, as we have seen, it is very easy to give false information about oneself. Only the domain name is reliable because it is detected by the server.

Always check a nickname with the /whois command which will provide more precise and more reliable information.

Notification

/notify

List of users you will be
notified about when they join
the network.

User's nickname.

Adds the nickname
to the notify list.

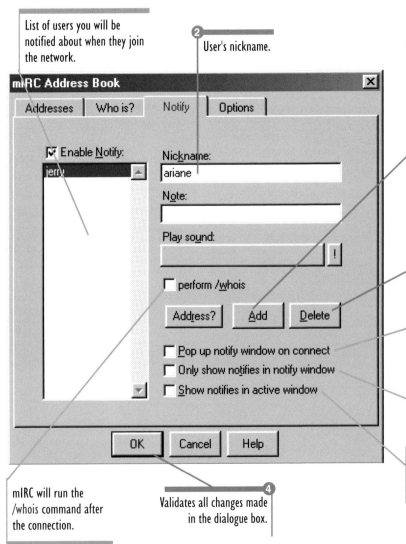

mIRC Address Book

Addresses | Who is? | Notify | Options

☑ Enable Notify:

jerry

Nickname:
ariane

Note:

Play sound:

☐ perform /whois

Address? | Add | Delete

☐ Pop up notify window on connect
☐ Only show notifies in notify window
☐ Show notifies in active window

OK | Cancel | Help

Deletes the selected
nickname from the list.

The Notify List window
will open and you will be
informed by a message
in the Status window.

Only the Notify List
window will open.

Only the notify message
will be displayed in the
Status window.

mIRC will run the
/whois command after
the connection.

Validates all changes made
in the dialogue box.

Checklist

1 Click on the Notify tab.

2 Enter the nickname
of a user if you wish to
be notified when s/he
connects to and
disconnects from the
IRC network.

3 Add it to your list.

4 Click OK to save
changes.

Hint

Always activate the perform
/whois option because
the nicknames are not reserved
for a particular user. Anyone
can connect under
any nickname.

Communicate
The channel window

Communication in a channel is always public. The messages you enter are read (in theory) by all the participants in the channel. Similarly, the channel window displays all the messages from the other participants.

You can choose from several types of messages:
- chat messages;
- action messages;
- away from keyboard messages (to get a bite to eat, for instance);
- parting messages when quitting a channel.

If the channel is very busy, the chat quickly becomes a hotch-potch of questions, answers and interjections, and it is, at times, difficult to know who is replying to whom. To clarify the discussion a bit, you can filter the messages to hide participants who do not interest you. You can also isolate the channel to chat privately with one of the participants.

HOW TO

If you want to talk to one participant in particular, start your message with his or her nickname followed by a colon.

peter : are you sure ?

TIPs

See page 20 for the rules of good conduct (etiquette) in IRC channels.

See also page 183 for an introduction to IRC jargon.

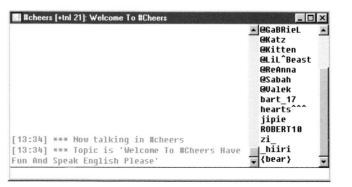

```
#cheers [+tnl 21]: Welcome To #Cheers                    _ □ ×
                                                    @GaBRieL
                                                    @Katz
                                                    @Kitten
                                                    @LiL^Beast
                                                    @ReAnna
                                                    @Sabah
                                                    @Valek
                                                    bart_17
                                                    hearts^^^
                                                    jipie
                                                    ROBERT10
[13:34] *** Now talking in #cheers                  zi_
[13:34] *** Topic is 'Welcome To #Cheers Have        _hiiri
Fun And Speak English Please'                       {bear}
```

Send

messages

Chatting

Type the text and press **Enter**.

An action message

Enter the command **/me** followed by the message.

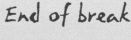

Take a break

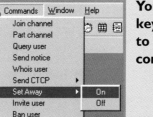

You are away from your keyboard and send a message to the users who may want to contact you.

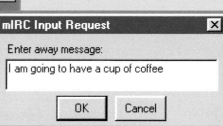

End of break

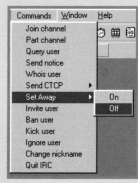

Change nickname

Commands | Window
- Join channel
- Part channel
- Query user
- Send notice
- Whois user
- Send CTCP
- Set Away
- Invite user
- Ban user
- Kick user
- Ignore user
- **Change nickname**
- Quit IRC

mIRC Input Request [×]

Enter new nickname:

jopp

[OK] [Cancel]

Send a private message

Enter the command /msg followed by the user's nickname and the message.

#windows [+tnl 35]: Windows & mIRC help channel. Ask your... [_][□][×]
www.download.com
[09:38] <jb1115> i get very strange
crashes lately :o[
[09:38] <aRJAy> lo Blue
/msg Peter Tomorrow then ?

@Aphobia
@Aqua
@BigDaddy
@BigMaMa

Leave the channel

Commands | Window
- Join channel
- **Part channel**
- Query user
- Send notice
- Whois user
- Send CTCP
- Set Away
- Invite user
- Ban user
- Kick user
- Ignore user
- Change nickname
- Quit IRC

mIRC Input Request [×]

Enter channel name:

Bye friends

[OK] [Cancel]

Invite a user

Commands | Window
- Join channel
- Part channel
- Query user
- Send notice
- Whois user
- Send CTCP ▸
- Set Away ▸
- **Invite user**
- Ban user
- Kick user
- Ignore user
- Change nick
- Quit IRC

This message is not seen by the other users.

mIRC Input Request [×]

Enter nickname and channel:

pierre #marabout

[OK] [Cancel]

The users to whom you send a private message (/msg) or a query (/query) need not necessarily participate in the same channel as yourself.

Request a private chat

DCC/Chat

① Enter the nickname of the user with whom you want to have a private (DCC) chat.

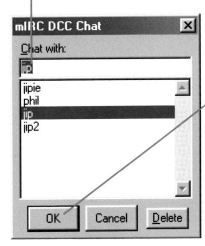

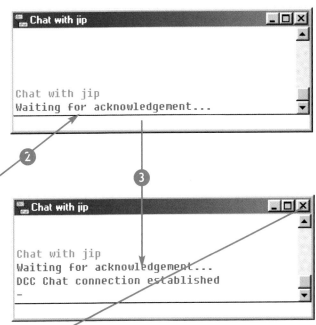

To end a DCC Chat session, just close the window.

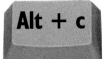
Alt + c

Select a user on the right pane of a channel window.
Click with the right mouse button.
Send a private (DCC) chat request with the **DCC/Chat** command.

Checklist

Select the **DCC/Chat** command.

① Enter the name of the user or select it from the list.

② Click OK and wait for his or her reply.

③ Your selected user accepts. Type your messages.

This chat is in theory totally private as it does not go through any channel. The two users are connected directly through their respective servers.

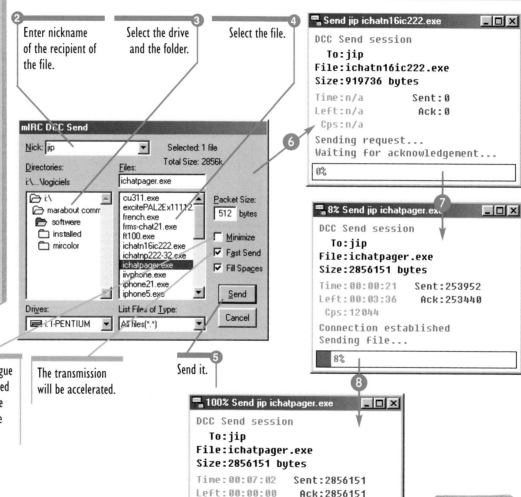
Checklist

1. Select the DCC/Send command.

2. Enter the recipient's nickname.

3. Select the drive and folder where the file is located.

4. Select the file.

5. Send it.

6. Wait for the recipient's acceptance.

7. The file is sent.

8. The transmission is ended.

② Enter nickname of the recipient of the file.

③ Select the drive and the folder.

④ Select the file.

```
Send jip ichatn16ic222.exe
DCC Send session
  To:jip
File:ichatn16ic222.exe
Size:919736 bytes
Time:n/a          Sent:0
Left:n/a          Ack:0
 Cps:n/a
Sending request...
Waiting for acknowledgement...
0%
```

mIRC DCC Send

Nick: jip
Selected: 1 file
Total Size: 2856k

Directories:
i:\...\logiciels

Files:
ichatpager.exe

📁 i:\
📂 marabout comm
📂 software
📁 installed
📁 mircolor

cu311.exe
excitePAL2Ex11112.
french.exe
frms-chat21.exe
ft100.exe
ichatn16ic222.exe
ichatnp222-32.exe
ichatpager.exe
iivphone.exe
iphone21.exe
iphone5.exe

Packet Size:
512 bytes

☐ Minimize
☑ Fast Send
☑ Fill Spaces

Drives:
i:\ I-PENTIUM

List Files of Type:
All files(*.*)

Send
Cancel

The DCC Send dialogue box will be minimised automatically at the beginning of the file transmission.

The transmission will be accelerated.

⑤ Send it.

```
8% Send jip ichatpager.exe
DCC Send session
  To:jip
File:ichatpager.exe
Size:2856151 bytes
Time:00:00:21    Sent:253952
Left:00:03:36    Ack:253440
 Cps:12044
Connection established
Sending file...
8%
```

```
100% Send jip ichatpager.exe
DCC Send session
  To:jip
File:ichatpager.exe
Size:2856151 bytes
Time:00:07:02    Sent:2856151
Left:00:00:00    Ack:2856151
 Cps:6768
Sending file...
DCC Send completed
```

If the transfer stops before the end, send the file again; the procedure will resume where it was interrupted.

Alt + s

The messages you receive

In a new window

```
#marabout                    _ □ ✕


<jip> We are dining together tonight
```

This is a private message. This window (similar to a Query window) opened automatically. The jip tab at the top of the mIRC window appeared in red.

In the channel window

```
<jip> hi jip
* jip I take a break
+++ jip is now known as jopp
+++ jip (jip@18-68.easynet.co.uk) has left #marabout
(bye bye)
```

A public standard message.
An action message sent by jip.
A message from the server.
A message from the server to inform you that jip is leaving the channel.

You are not informed if somebody requests information about you (/whois).

If one of the participants is too noisy, vulgar, aggressive or annoying, you can prevent his or her messages from being displayed. Select the Commands/Ignore command. Enter the nickname of the user to be ignored.

In the Status window

```
*** jip (jip@18-68.CampusNet.ucl.ac.be) invites you to join
#marabout
[jip PING]
```

Message from the server: you are invited to join the #marabout channel. The jip user has sent you the CTCP Ping command.

You can also click with the right mouse button on the user selected beforehand in the channel window. Select the Ignore command.

```
mIRC Input Request              ✕
Enter nickname:
pol
              OK      Cancel
```

Notes

After a warning message, you can accept or decline the file being sent to you.

The progress of the transfer is displayed.

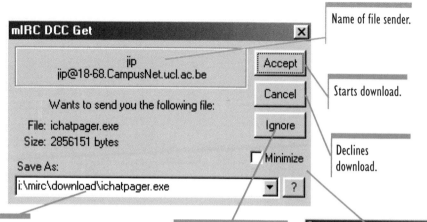

Name of file sender.

Starts download.

Declines download.

Accepts the location of the download or selects another one.

Declines download and all new offers of files for the next thirty seconds.

This dialogue box appears if the sender resends a file whose downloading was interrupted or if the sender sends a file with the same name as a file which already exists in the folder of your hard disc.

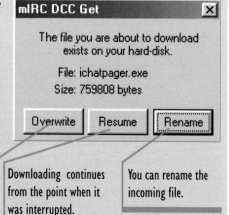

The incoming file overwrites the existing file.

Downloading continues from the point when it was interrupted.

You can rename the incoming file.

Hint
Accept only files from reliable users, and always run the anti-virus program on them.

Receive a chat request

Note

When you receive a chat request, you can:
- accept;
- decline;
- decline for the moment – all new requests will subsequently be automatically rejected for the next 30 seconds.

The user jip requests a private (DCC) chat (DCC Chat)

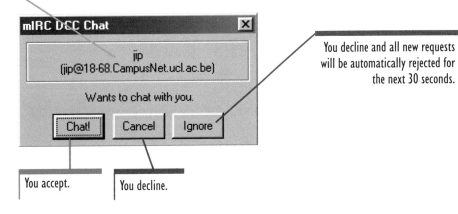

You decline and all new requests will be automatically rejected for the next 30 seconds.

You accept.

You decline.

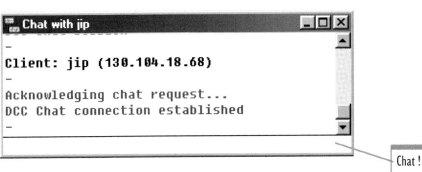

Chat !

Flow chart of DCC chat commands

You request a chat

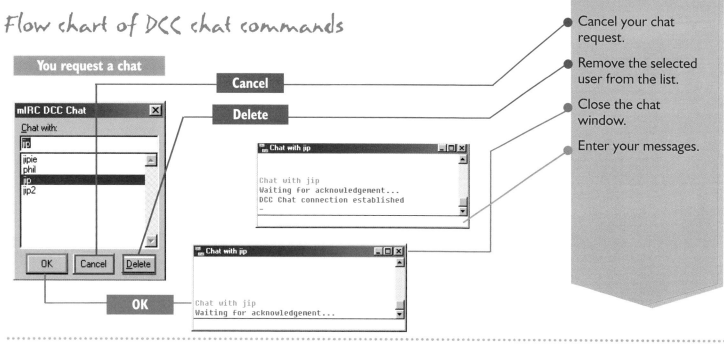

- Cancel your chat request.
- Remove the selected user from the list.
- Close the chat window.
- Enter your messages.

Cancel

Delete

OK

You receive a chat request

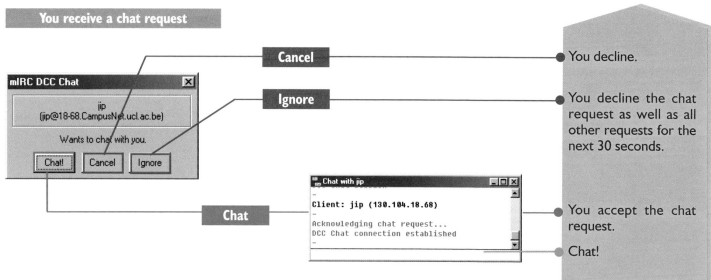

Cancel → You decline.

Ignore → You decline the chat request as well as all other requests for the next 30 seconds.

Chat → You accept the chat request.

Chat!

DCC file command flow chart

You send a file

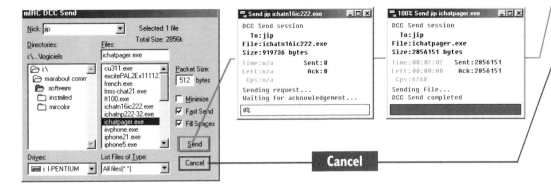

Cancel

- Send a file: it is accepted and transmitted.

- Close the dialogue box without sending anything.

You receive a file

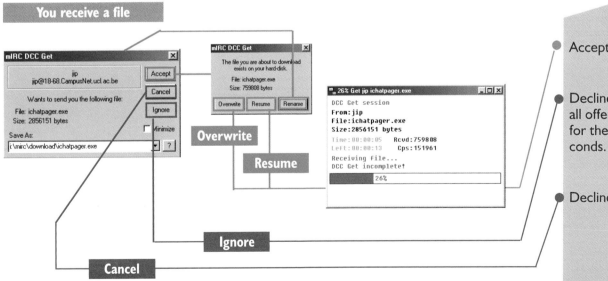

Overwrite

Resume

Ignore

Cancel

- Accept the file.

- Decline the offer and all offers to send files for the next 30 seconds.

- Decline the file.

You are the operator

Commands/Join Channel

Yes, you can be the operator (the boss actually) of a channel. All you have to do is join a channel whose name does not yet exist on the server. You automatically become the channel operator: your nickname is preceded by the @ sign in the right pane of the channel window.

As a channel operator, you can change the operating mode of the channel, kick, op or de-op a user, and so on.

The channel will close automatically and disappear as soon as the last user has left, so it is not permanent. You must create it again every time you connect.

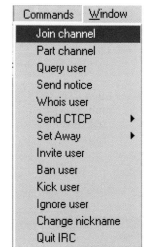

HOW TO

Open the list of your favourite channels by clicking on the Channel folders button.

Enter the name of the channel you wish to create every time you connect.

Validate the option: Pop up folder on connect.

Next time you connect, you will simply have to click on the name of your channel to create it.

CHAPTER 1 : MIRC

57

Channel settings

Channel Modes

Channel modes.

Topic.

Ban list.

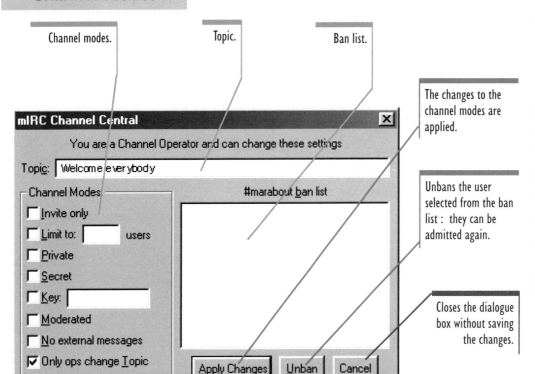

mIRC Channel Central

You are a Channel Operator and can change these settings

Topic: | Welcome everybody |

Channel Modes
- ☐ Invite only
- ☐ Limit to: [ ] users
- ☐ Private
- ☐ Secret
- ☐ Key: [ ]
- ☐ Moderated
- ☐ No external messages
- ☑ Only ops change Topic

#marabout ban list

[Apply Changes] [Unban] [Cancel]

The changes to the channel modes are applied.

Unbans the user selected from the ban list : they can be admitted again.

Closes the dialogue box without saving the changes.

Option	Mode
Invite only	i
Limit to	l
Private	p
Secret	s
Key	k
Moderated	m
No external messages	n
Only ops change topic	t

Notes

Click on the background of the channel window with the right mouse button and select the Channel Modes command.

When you ban a user, his or her nickname is put on the ban list. This list is erased as soon as the channel is closed.

For an explanation of the modes, see page 17.

If you do not wish to be disturbed in a channel where you are the operator, validate the modes Invite only, Secret, No external messages, Key and Only ops change topic.

Control

Select the user in the right pane of the channel window.

Select the command to apply to this user from the Control menu.

The user is kicked out of the channel but can rejoin it immediately.

The user is opped: s/he gets operator status.

The user is deopped: s/he loses operator status.

The user is kicked out and receives a message explaining why s/he was kicked out.

The user is kicked out and banned from the channel.

The user is put on the ban list. See page 58. S/he is not kicked out, but once out of the channel, s/he can no longer rejoin it.

To ban an unwelcome user from your channel, apply the BanKick command on that user. His/her nickname will be automatically put on the ban list (see page 58).

Chapter 2

IRCle

Introducing IRCle

This is the best known **IRC** software in the **Macintosh** world.
Publisher: Mac Response
Publisher's website: http://www.ircle.com
Shareware
System requirements:
Mac 68 K or Power Mac with System 7.0 at least (preferably System 8)
MacTCP as of version 2.0.x or Open Transport 1.1 at least
Download from: http://www.ircle.com/download.html (1,1 Mo)

Visit the following sites for additional information, tips, and hints:
http://www.eskimo.com/~pristine/irclem.html
http://www.aloha.net/~sputnik/irclehelp.html

TIP

What can you do with the IRCle ?

Connect simultaneously to several servers
and several networks.
Consult and filter a channels list.
Send and receive private and public messages.
Ignore unwelcome users.
Obtain information on the users of a channel.
Establish a DCC connection for a private (DCC) chat
and to send messages.
Create your own channel and have full control
over it.
Record and print a chat.

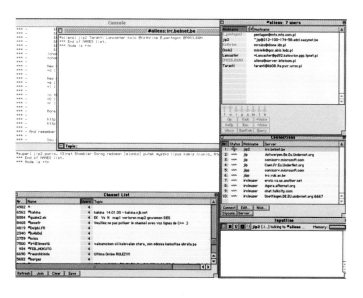

Connect

When you connect for the first time, you must indicate the name of the server and enter your personal details: your name, nickname, and e-mail address.

You can configure 10 connections that will then be at your disposal. If, for example, a server rejects your connection, you can call another one immediately.

You can even connect simultaneously to several servers in the same network or in different networks.

HOW TO

1: ⊞
2: ↗↙
3: ←→

1. The attempt to connect failed.
2. The connection was not attempted.
3. The connection is established.

TIP

You can connect simultaneously to several servers in several networks. Multiple connections to the same network (known as clones) through different servers enable you to remain present in the network even if there is a split. But clones are not generally well thought of and often prohibited.

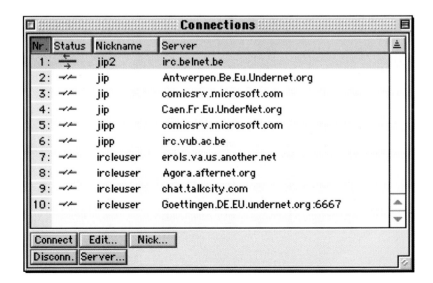

Nr.	Status	Nickname	Server
1:	←→	jip2	irc.belnet.be
2:	↗↙	jip	Antwerpen.Be.Eu.Undernet.org
3:	↗↙	jip	comicsrv.microsoft.com
4:	↗↙	jip	Caen.Fr.Eu.UnderNet.org
5:	↗↙	jipp	comicsrv.microsoft.com
6:	↗↙	jipp	irc.vub.ac.be
7:	↗↙	ircleuser	erols.va.us.another.net
8:	↗↙	ircleuser	Agora.afternet.org
9:	↗↙	ircleuser	chat.talkcity.com
10:	↗↙	ircleuser	Goettingen.DE.EU.undernet.org:6667

Connections

Connect · Edit... · Nick...
Disconn. · Server...

The Connections window

Windows/Connections

Note

The Connections window is normally displayed automatically when you start IRCle.

If it is not visible, display it with the Windows/ Connections command.

Ten (preset) connections are ready to use.

Click on a title to sort the 10 connections according to the contents of one of the columns.

Connects to the server defined in the selected connection.

Disconnects from the server selected from the list.

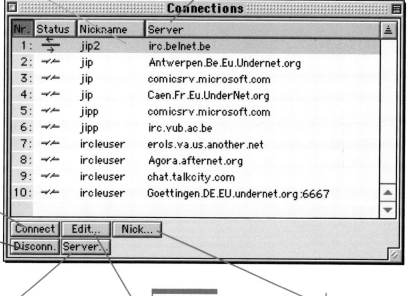

Nr.	Status	Nickname	Server
1:		jip2	irc.belnet.be
2:		jip	Antwerpen.Be.Eu.Undernet.org
3:		jip	comicsrv.microsoft.com
4:		jip	Caen.Fr.Eu.UnderNet.org
5:		jipp	comicsrv.microsoft.com
6:		jipp	irc.vub.ac.be
7:		ircleuser	erols.va.us.another.net
8:		ircleuser	Agora.afternet.org
9:		ircleuser	chat.talkcity.com
10:		ircleuser	Goettingen.DE.EU.undernet.org:6667

Connect   Edit...   Nick...
Disconn.   Server.

Opens the servers list.

Defines and changes the settings of the selected connection.

Changes nickname.

 +

Connection settings

Edit button

① Select a server (see page 68).

② Enter your nickname.

③ Enter the name that identifies you on the Internet.

④ Some servers require a password to connect.

⑤ Enter some information that describes you.

⑥ Click to save the settings.

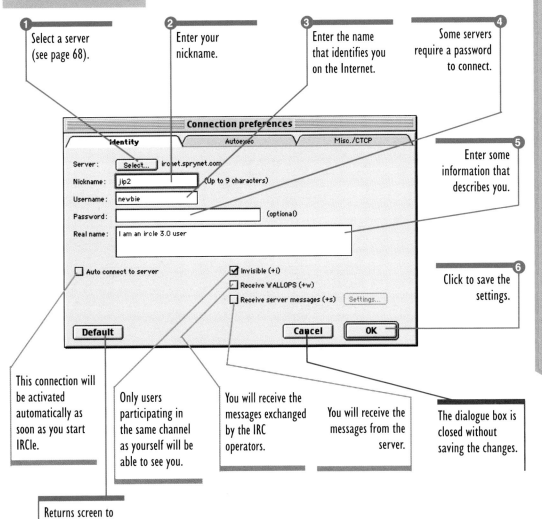

Connection preferences

| Identity | Autoexec | Misc./CTCP |

Server: [Select...] irchet.sprynet.com

Nickname: [jip2] (Up to 9 characters)

Username: [newbie]

Password: [ ] (optional)

Real name: [I am an ircle 3.0 user]

☐ Auto connect to server

☑ Invisible (+i)
☐ Receive WALLOPS (+w)
☐ Receive server messages (+s) [Settings...]

[Default]   [Cancel] [OK]

This connection will be activated automatically as soon as you start IRCle.

Returns screen to default settings

Only users participating in the same channel as yourself will be able to see you.

You will receive the messages exchanged by the IRC operators.

You will receive the messages from the server.

The dialogue box is closed without saving the changes.

Checklist

① Select a server.

② Enter your nickname.

③ Enter your logon name.

④ Enter the password (if required by the server).

⑤ Enter some information that describes you (but nothing too personal).

⑥ Click on OK.

Once you have changed the settings of a connection, to keep them permanently, record them with the File/Save preferences command.

Hint

All the information you enter here can be seen by the other users. Be careful: it might be preferable not to give your real name.

Notes

Click on the Edit button in the Connections window, and then click on the Autoexec tab.

See the list of commands on page 14.

The Misc./CTCP button contains the option to enter your e-mail.

Enter the commands that will be carried out automatically as soon as the connection is established.

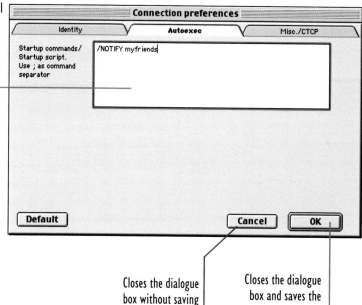

Closes the dialogue box without saving the changes.

Closes the dialogue box and saves the options.

Separate the different commands by a semicolon.
Example : /join #marabout;/notify pol
You will join the #marabout channel
and you will be informed when pol connects to the server.

Servers

Server button

List of servers.

Changes the settings of the selected server.

Closes the window without saving the changes.

The server pointed to in the list is selected for the connection activated in the Connections window.

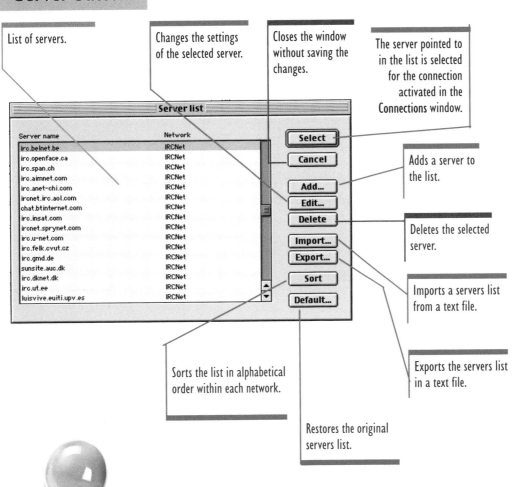

Adds a server to the list.

Deletes the selected server.

Imports a servers list from a text file.

Exports the servers list in a text file.

Sorts the list in alphabetical order within each network.

Restores the original servers list.

Delete from the list servers which are not relevant to you.

Notes

Click on the **Server** button in the Connections window.

When you add a server, enter its address, port (usually 6667 will do) and select the network to which it belongs.

Warning

When you restore the original servers list, those you have entered yourself will be lost.

Notes

When connected, the server sends you the message of the day (MOTD).

You can display the message of the day later with the /motd command.

If the nickname you have chosen is already used by someone else on the network, you will have to choose a new one and try a new connection.

Name of computer housing the IRC server and server software version.

Date and time of last startup of server.

Number of users connected to the network and number of servers in the network.

Number of server operators (IRCop) connected.

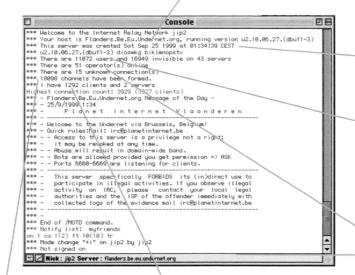

Number of chat channels accessible on the network.

Number of clients (i.e. computers like yours) connected to the server.

Your nickname and the name of the server.

Connections window flow chart

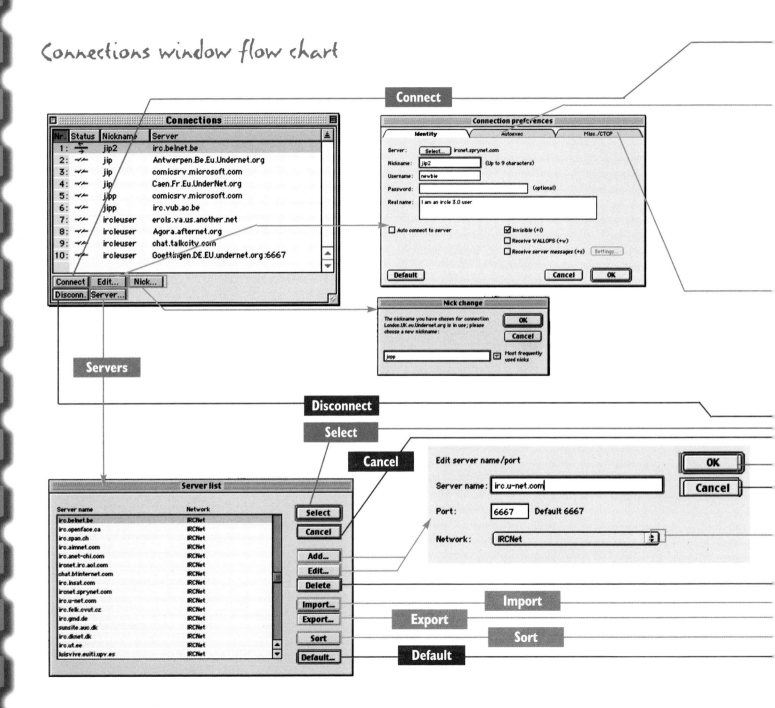

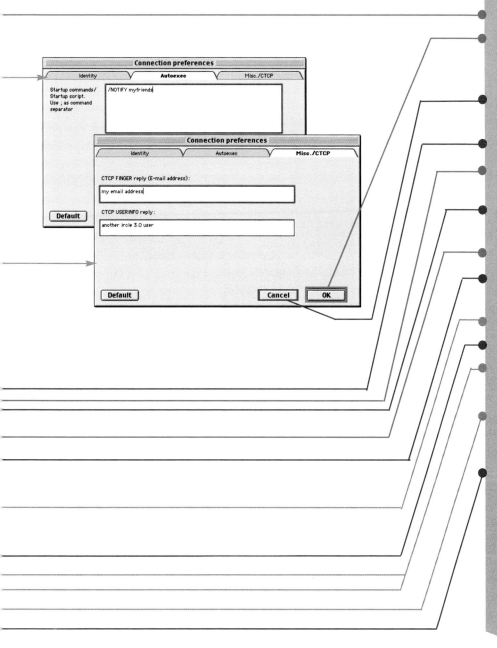

Connects to selected server.

Saves all the settings (the three tabs) of the dialogue box.

Closes the dialogue box without saving the changes.

Disconnects from the selected server.

The selected server becomes the default server.

Closes the dialogue box without saving the changes.

Saves the new nickname.

Closes the dialogue box without saving the new nickname.

Selects a network.

Deletes the selected server.

Imports or exports the servers list into or from a text file.

Sorts the servers list in alphabetical order in each network.

Restores the default servers list. All your changes will be lost.

Join a channel

Every network is independent of the others and offers specific channels. The name, therefore, is not enough in itself to join a given channel: you must also know the network in which this channel is located.

Once you have joined a channel, you are immediately in communication with the other participants in this channel. You may be refused entry into a channel for various reasons:
- you must be invited by a participant in the channel;
- a password is required;
- you are in the channel's ban list;
- the maximum number of participants has been reached.

HOW TO
Enter a channel either with the **Commands/Join** command or by clicking twice on the name of the channel in the Channels List window.

TIP

If the cs list hannelwindow is no longer displayed on the screen, do not use the Commands/List command, but rather the Windows/Channels List command. The list will be restored.

#marabout: sprynet.us.galaxynet.org

```
#marabout: @jip2
*** End of /NAMES list.
*** Mode is +
*** Channel created at october 28  10:48:55  1999
*** jip2 has set the topic on channel #marabout to computer books
```

Topic: computer books **set by**: jip2 **on**: 28/10/99 10:50:38

Checklist

1. Select the Commands/List command.

2. Tick the options for the channels you want to see in the list.

3. If you are connected to several servers, select the one you are interested in.

4. Click on OK to have the list built on the basis of the filtering criteria of the dialogue window.

Warning

Entering a value for the options minimum of users, maximum of users and matching is not enough. You must also tick the checkbox.

Which channels are available ?

Commands/List

Select the server you are interested in.

Click to have the list built.

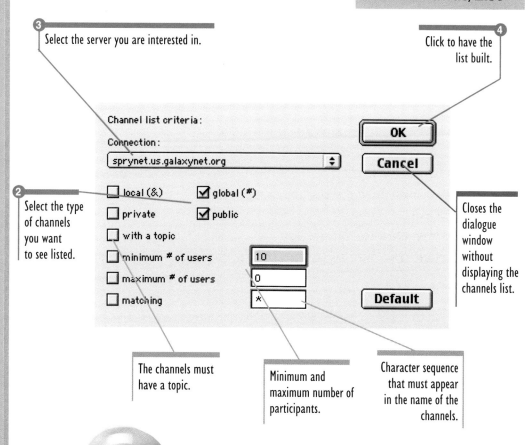

Channel list criteria:

Connection:

sprynet.us.galaxynet.org

OK

Cancel

Closes the dialogue window without displaying the channels list.

☐ local (&)   ☑ global (#)

Select the type of channels you want to see listed.

☐ private   ☑ public

☐ with a topic

☐ minimum # of users   10

☐ maximum # of users   0

☐ matching   *

Default

The channels must have a topic.

Minimum and maximum number of participants.

Character sequence that must appear in the name of the channels.

The global channels are offered by all the servers of the same network. The local channels are specific to a server.

The private channels are assigned from the p mode (see page 17).

The channels list

Commands/List

Click on a column title to sort the channels according to the contents of this column.

Name of channels.

Number of participants.

Topic.

Closes the window.

Update the list through the criteria dialogue box.

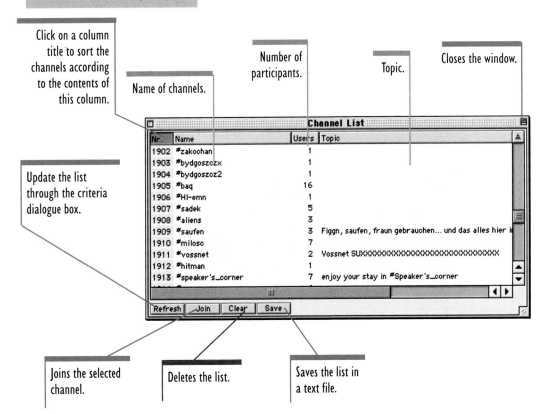

Joins the selected channel.

Deletes the list.

Saves the list in a text file.

Click the OK button in the dialogue box Channel list criteria.

The list may take some time (several minutes) to build because there are thousands of channels.

Reverse the sorting order (increasing or decreasing) by clicking on the title of the columns.

Checklist

1. If you are connected to several networks, select the server.

2. Enter the name of the channel and do not forget the # or & sign.

3. Click on OK to join the channel.

   You can participate in several channels simultaneously.

Come right in !

Commands/Join

If several connections are active, select the server.

Enter the name of the channel (preceded by # or &).

Click to join the channel.

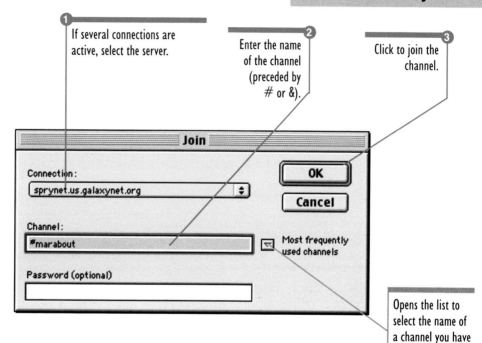

Join

Connection :

sprynet.us.galaxynet.org

Channel :

#marabout

Password (optional)

OK

Cancel

Most frequently used channels

Opens the list to select the name of a channel you have accessed before.

Save time. When you have joined a channel, save the name of the channel and the name of the server with the command File/Create .chat file.

All you then have to do is click twice on the icon of this document to open the IRCle, connect to the server and join the channel.

 +

CHAPTER 2 : IRCLE

75

Chat !

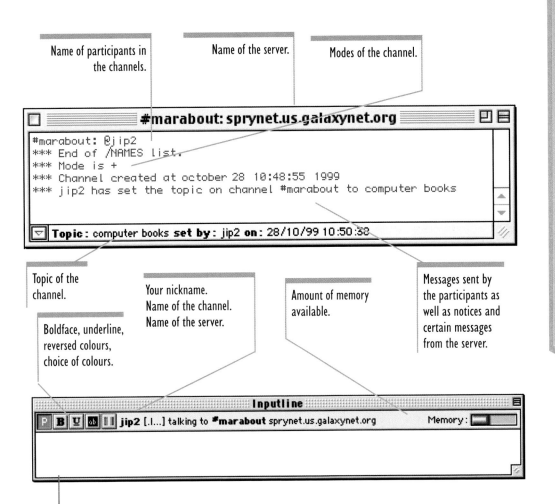

Name of participants in the channels.

Name of the server.

Modes of the channel.

```
#marabout: sprynet.us.galaxynet.org          □ ▤
#marabout: @jip2
*** End of /NAMES list.
*** Mode is +
*** Channel created at october 28 10:48:55 1999
*** jip2 has set the topic on channel #marabout to computer books  ▲
                                                                    ▼
▽ Topic: computer books set by: jip2 on: 28/10/99 10:50:38
```

Topic of the channel.

Boldface, underline, reversed colours, choice of colours.

Your nickname.
Name of the channel.
Name of the server.

Amount of memory available.

Messages sent by the participants as well as notices and certain messages from the server.

```
                          Inputline                              ▤
P B U ab ▌▌ jip2 [.I...] talking to #marabout sprynet.us.galaxynet.org    Memory: ▭▭
```

Enter your messages and commands and press Enter to send them.

If the window of the channel is invisible, activate it: open the Window menu and select the channel you are interested in from the bottom of the menu.

Notes

The channel window displays the results of the commands and messages from the server in relation to the channel.

Your messages will be visible to all the participants in the channel.

Warning

The Inputline window is common to all the channels. Activate the window of the channel in which you want to intervene before sending the message or command you have typed in the Inputline window.

who is there ?

When you join a channel, the IRC server provides a list of the users present (in the channel window). Only the nicknames are displayed.

A nickname does not really provide any significant information. The **Participants** window displays the name of the host computer from which each is connected to the Internet, but you can obtain more precise details on each user by using the **/whois** command. Similarly, it is very easy to find out that user's response time by sending him or her a ping command.

TIP
Do not rely on the information provided by the users because, as we have seen, it is very easy to give just any information on oneself. Only the domain name is reliable because it is detected by the server.

HOW TO
With the /who command followed by the name of the channel, the server provides some summary information on the users: their nickname, status, logon name and IP address.

H (Here): the user is connected to the IRC network and is active.

G (Gone): the user is connected but is not actively involved in his or her session.

*: the user is an IRC operator (IRCop).

@: the user is a channel operator (op).

```
#swiss_cottage: sprynet.us.galaxynet.org

#swiss_cottage: JiP2 KriSFlyer XuHn`XuHn TuRbU|v| FReaK Usky UzHaK-BoT [iCy`kEn] BaBYSmUrf gIr|gErl5
PoLo_Ga| y0z|3 SiAojAcKi @GTO^AWAY
*** End of /NAMES list.
*** Mode is +
*** Channel created at october 28  8:35:13 1999
-*OzHaK-BoT*- 2 Hi and welcome to  #swiss_cottage 2 This is 2 OzH 2K BoT  version 1.1a 3 Please type
games 3 in the channel to select a game.  Also Please visit my Web Page at 2
http://www.ozhakz.cjb.net
*** GTO^AWAY is now known as LoVe^GtO
```
Topic : where's Q!!??? ======>Q has arrive pls tell SiAojAcKi!! set by : SiAojAcKi on : 28/10/99 10:59:36

The users window

Windows/Users

Click on the title of a column to sort the list or change the sorting order (increasing or decreasing).

Name of the channel and the number of participants (including robots).

Invisible participants (+i mode).

Name of the host computer of the participants.

Notes

Select the **Windows/Users** command.

If a nickname is in red, it is that of an operator or a robot.

This window displays the list of participants in the channel whose window is active.

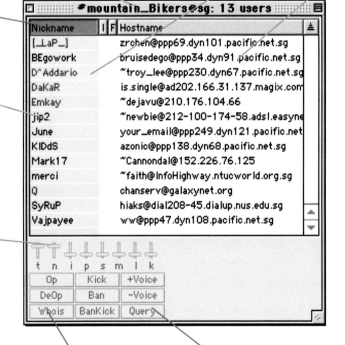

Nickname of the participants.

Modes of the channel (here: + t + n).

The buttons represent commands reserved for the operators.

Obtain the identity of the selected user (see page 79).

Open a direct connection with the selected user (see page 88).

Users identity

Whois button

Notes

Select the name of the user from the Users window, then click on the Whois button.

To obtain the response time of a participant: select the user in the Participants window and click on the Cping button.

If no participant is selected in the window, they are all "pinged."

If the Cping button is absent, you can add it with the **File/Preferences** command (Buttons tab).

Name of the user.

Channels in which the user participates.

Name of the host computer (host name) from which the user is connected.

```
#mountain_Bikers@sg: sprynet.us.galaxynet.org
*** jip2 is ~newbie@212-100-174-58.adsl.easynet.be (I am an ircle 3.0 user)
*** jip2 is on channels #mountain_Bikers@sg
*** jip2 is on IRC via server sprynet.us.galaxynet.org (No Man Is An Island)
*** jip2 has been idle for 16 minutes and 0 seconds
*** jip2 signed on at october 28  8:35:13 1999
Topic : Sunday BT Carpark 10am, bring BIKE Going: Emkay, zul,PaLmEr,BruisedEGO, R32 , (add on) [th
```

Server to which the user is connected.

The Commands/Whois command inserts /whois in the Input window. Complete by inserting the nickname.

Users window tree

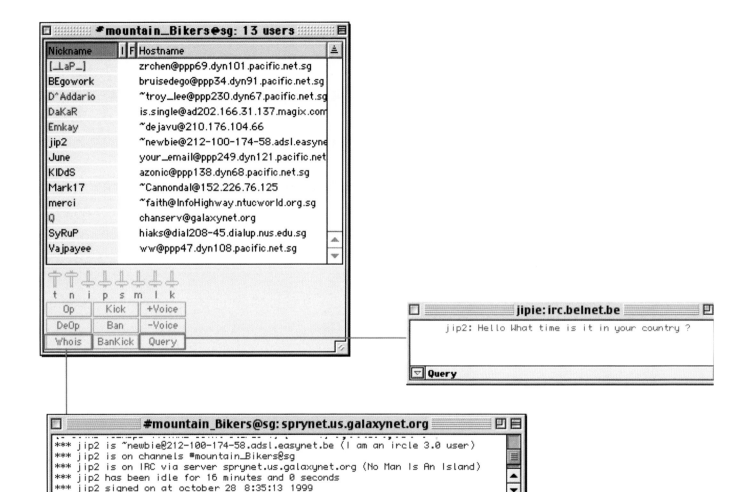

The windows

The messages from the server are displayed in the active window : the **Console** window or a channel window, whereas messages exchanged in a channel are in a specific window (one per channel).

The **Participants** window, on the other hand, is unique: it displays the participants in the active channel.

The **Console** window and the channel windows function in a standard manner, like all **Macintosh** windows. They also offer common fields and commands for, e.g. saving all the data in a file as they are displayed.

The title of the window always gives all the necessary particulars for identifying the information displayed in it.

HOW TO

Print the contents of the Console window and the channel windows with the File/Print command.

TIP

The list of available windows is given in the Windows menu.

It is therefore very easy to bring back to the foreground a window lost in the stacking.

Windows	
Cycle	⌘,
✓ Console	⌘-
✓ Users	⌘U
DCC status	⌘D
Faces	⌘F
✓ Connections	⌘K
✓ Channel list	⌘L
Tile channels	⌘T
Tile channels+Console	⌥⌘T
Stack windows	
9: #marabout	

The Console window

Windows/Console

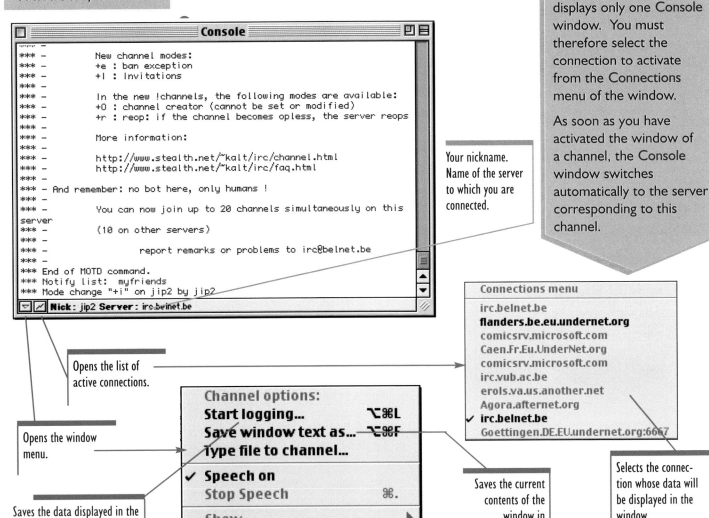

Notes

Even if several connections are active, the IRCle displays only one Console window. You must therefore select the connection to activate from the Connections menu of the window.

As soon as you have activated the window of a channel, the Console window switches automatically to the server corresponding to this channel.

```
                              Console
*** -          New channel modes:
*** -          +e : ban exception
*** -          +I : Invitations
*** -
*** -          In the new !channels, the following modes are available:
*** -          +O : channel creator (cannot be set or modified)
*** -          +r : reop: if the channel becomes opless, the server reops
*** -
*** -          More information:
*** -
*** -          http://www.stealth.net/~kalt/irc/channel.html
*** -          http://www.stealth.net/~kalt/irc/faq.html
*** -
*** - And remember: no bot here, only humans !
*** -
*** -          You can now join up to 20 channels simultaneously on this
server
*** -          (10 on other servers)
*** -
*** -                 report remarks or problems to irc@belnet.be
*** -
*** - End of MOTD command.
*** Notify list: myfriends
*** Mode change "+i" on jip2 by jip2
Nick : jip2 Server : irc.belnet.be
```

Your nickname. Name of the server to which you are connected.

Opens the list of active connections.

Connections menu

irc.belnet.be
flanders.be.eu.undernet.org
comicsrv.microsoft.com
Caen.Fr.Eu.UnderNet.org
comicsrv.microsoft.com
irc.vub.ac.be
erols.va.us.another.net
Agora.afternet.org
✓ **irc.belnet.be**
Goettingen.DE.EU.undernet.org:6667

Opens the window menu.

Channel options:
Start logging...   ⌥⌘L
Save window text as...   ⌥⌘F
Type file to channel...

✓ **Speech on**
   Stop Speech   ⌘.

   Show   ▶
   Color protocol   ▶

Saves the data displayed in the window gradually in a text file.

Saves the current contents of the window in a text file.

Selects the connection whose data will be displayed in the window.

Notes

The Show menu displays specific messages:

Join: newcomers to the channel.

Part: departure of participants.

Sign off: the participants who disconnect from the server.

Mode changes: changes of channel mode.

Kick: banned participants.

Nick changes: the change of nickname of the participants.

Windows

You leave the channel.

Name of the channel and of the server.

Display of messages and results of commands regarding the channel.

Topic of the channel; author of the topic.

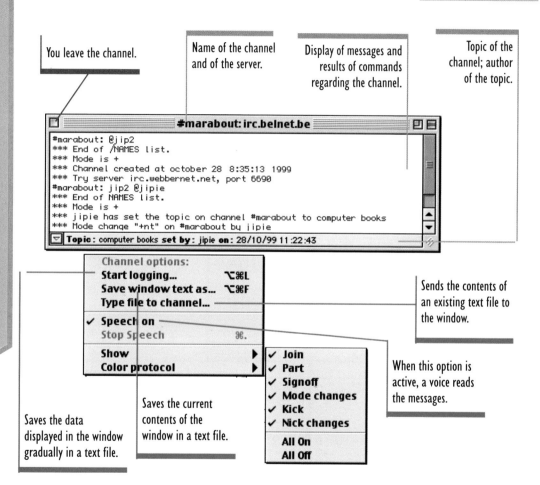

```
#marabout: @jip2
*** End of /NAMES list.
*** Mode is +
*** Channel created at october 28  8:35:13 1999
*** Try server irc.webbernet.net, port 6690
#marabout: jip2 @jipie
*** End of NAMES list.
*** Mode is +
*** jipie has set the topic on channel #marabout to computer books
*** Mode change "+nt" on #marabout by jipie
```
Topic: computer books set by: jipie on: 28/10/99 11:22:43

Channel options:
Start logging...   ⌥⌘L
Save window text as... ⌥⌘F
Type file to channel...

✓ Speech on
  Stop Speech   ⌘.

  Show   ►
  Color protocol   ►

✓ Join
✓ Part
✓ Signoff
✓ Mode changes
✓ Kick
✓ Nick changes
  All On
  All Off

Sends the contents of an existing text file to the window.

When this option is active, a voice reads the messages.

Saves the data displayed in the window gradually in a text file.

Saves the current contents of the window in a text file.

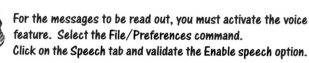

For the messages to be read out, you must activate the voice feature. Select the File/Preferences command.
Click on the Speech tab and validate the Enable speech option.

Managing the windows

Windows

Displays the window the photograph of participants in the active channel (provided they have submitted a photograph).

Moves the selected window to the background.

Restores the Console window to the foreground.

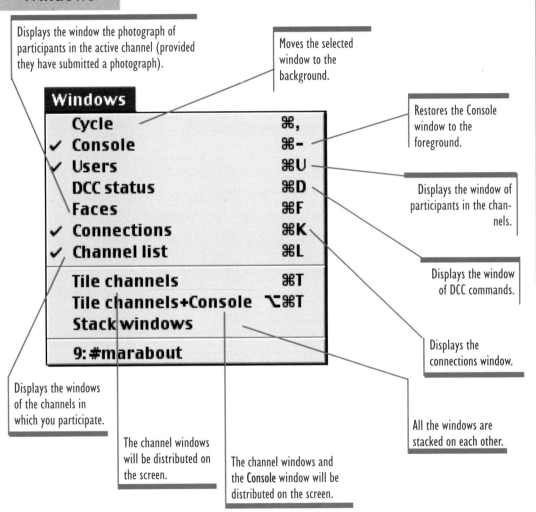

Windows

Cycle	⌘,
✓ Console	⌘-
✓ Users	⌘U
DCC status	⌘D
Faces	⌘F
✓ Connections	⌘K
✓ Channel list	⌘L
Tile channels	⌘T
Tile channels+Console	⌥⌘T
Stack windows	
9:#marabout	

Displays the window of participants in the channels.

Displays the window of DCC commands.

Displays the connections window.

Displays the windows of the channels in which you participate.

The channel windows will be distributed on the screen.

The channel windows and the **Console** window will be distributed on the screen.

All the windows are stacked on each other.

Notes

A window whose name is preceded by the √ symbol is open. Click on its name to restore it to the foreground.

A window whose name is not preceded by the √ symbol is not open. Click on its name to restore it to the foreground.

The Console window always remains open.

CHAPTER 2 : IRCLE

84

Communicate

Communication in a channel is always public. The messages you enter are read (in theory) by all the participants in the channel. Similarly, the channel window displays all the messages from the other participants.

You can choose from several types of message:
- chat messages;
- action messages;
- away from keyboard messages (to get a bite to eat, for instance);
- the parting message when quitting the channel.

If the channel is very busy, the chat quickly becomes a hotchpotch of questions, answers, and interjections and it is, at times, difficult to know who is replying to whom. To clarify the discussion a bit, you can filter the messages to hide users who do not interest you. You can also isolate the channel to chat privately with one of the participants.

TIPS

See page 20 for the rules
of good conduct (etiquette)
in IRC channels.
See also page 183 for an
introduction
to IRC jargon.

HOW TO

If you want to talk to one participant in particular, start your message with his or her nickname followed by a colon.

peter : are you sure ?

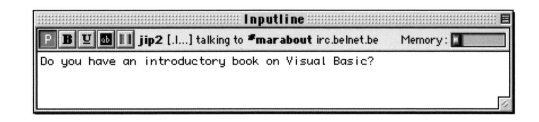

Send

messages

Chatting

Type the text and press Enter.

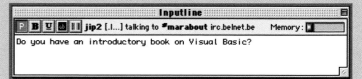

Taking a break

Commands/Away

You are away from your keyboard and send a message to the users.

The message.

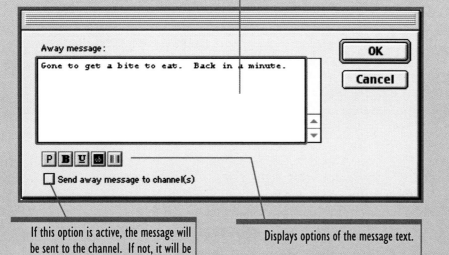

If this option is active, the message will be sent to the channel. If not, it will be sent only in reply to private messages.

Displays options of the message text.

End of break

Commands	
Join...	⌘J
Part...	
List...	
Who...	⌘O
Query...	⌘E
WhoIs...	⌘S
Invite...	⌘I
Kick...	
Away...	⌘Y
Message...	⌘M
DCC Send	⌥⌘D
DCC Chat	⌥⌘C

An action message

Enter the /me command followed by the message.

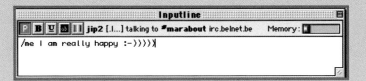

```
Inputline
P B U ab II  jip2 [.l...] talking to #marabout irc.belnet.be   Memory: ▮
/me I am really happy :-)))))|
```

Invite a user to chat

This message is not seen by the other users.

```
Commands
Join...       ⌘J
Part...
List...
Who...        ⌘O
Query...      ⌘E
WhoIs...      ⌘S
Invite...     ⌘I
Kick...
Away...       ⌘Y
Message...    ⌘M
DCC Send   ⌥⌘D
DCC Chat   ⌥⌘C
```

```
Inputline
P B U ab II  jip2 [.l...] talking to #marabout ... Memory: ▮
/invite phil #marabout
```

Leave the channel

Enter the name of the channel and your parting message.

```
Commands
Join...       ⌘J
Part...
List...
Who...        ⌘O
Query...      ⌘E
WhoIs...      ⌘S
Invite...     ⌘I
Kick...
Away...       ⌘Y
Message...    ⌘M
DCC Send   ⌥⌘D
DCC Chat   ⌥⌘C
```

```
Inputline
P B U ab II  jip2 [.l...] talking to (nobody) ...   Memory: ▮
/part #marabout a+|
```

Send messages

Send a private message

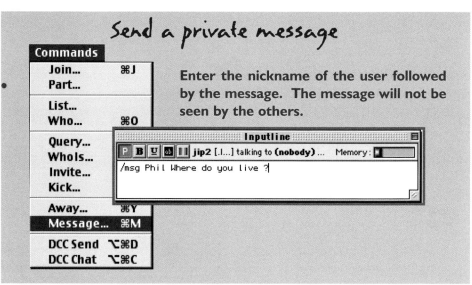

Enter the nickname of the user followed by the message. The message will not be seen by the others.

Commands

Join...	⌘J
Part...	
List...	
Who...	⌘O
Query...	
WhoIs...	
Invite...	
Kick...	
Away...	⌘Y
Message...	⌘M
DCC Send	⌥⌘D
DCC Chat	⌥⌘C

Inputline

/msg Phil Where do you live ?|

Send a private (DCC) chat request

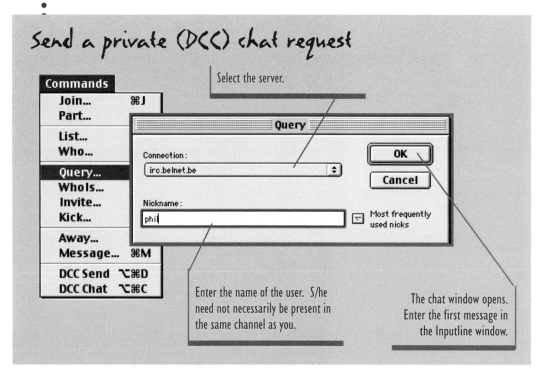

Commands

Join...	⌘J
Part...	
List...	
Who...	
Query...	
WhoIs...	
Invite...	
Kick...	
Away...	
Message...	⌘M
DCC Send	⌥⌘D
DCC Chat	⌥⌘C

Query

Connection:
irc.belnet.be

Nickname:
phil|

Most frequently used nicks

OK

Cancel

Select the server.

Enter the name of the user. S/he need not necessarily be present in the same channel as you.

The chat window opens. Enter the first message in the Inputline window.

The Query command is available in the Users window.

+Voice
-Voice
Query

Checklist

Select the **Commands/ DCC chat** command.

1. Select the server.

2. Enter the name of the user to whom you are sending the request.

3. Enter the request.

4. Wait for that user's reply.

5. Start to chat as soon as the chat window opens.

To end a DCC chat, just close the window.

When the other user leaves the chat session, you are informed by a message to that effect.

A private (DCC) chat

Commands/DCC Chat

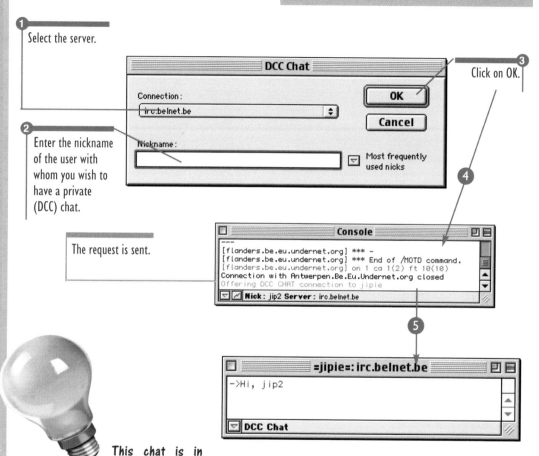

Select the server.

DCC Chat

Connection:
irc.belnet.be

OK

Cancel

Enter the nickname of the user with whom you wish to have a private (DCC) chat.

Nickname:

Most frequently used nicks

Click on OK.

The request is sent.

Console

[flanders.be.eu.undernet.org] *** -
[flanders.be.eu.undernet.org] *** End of /MOTD command.
[flanders.be.eu.undernet.org] on 1 ca 1(2) ft 10(10)
Connection with Antwerpen.Be.Eu.Undernet.org closed
Offering DCC CHAT connection to jipie

Nick: jip2 **Server:** irc.belnet.be

=jipie=:irc.belnet.be

->Hi, jip2

DCC Chat

This chat is in theory totally private as it does not go through any channel. The two users are connected directly through their respective servers.

CHAPTER 2 : IRCLE

89

Send a file

Commands/DCC Send

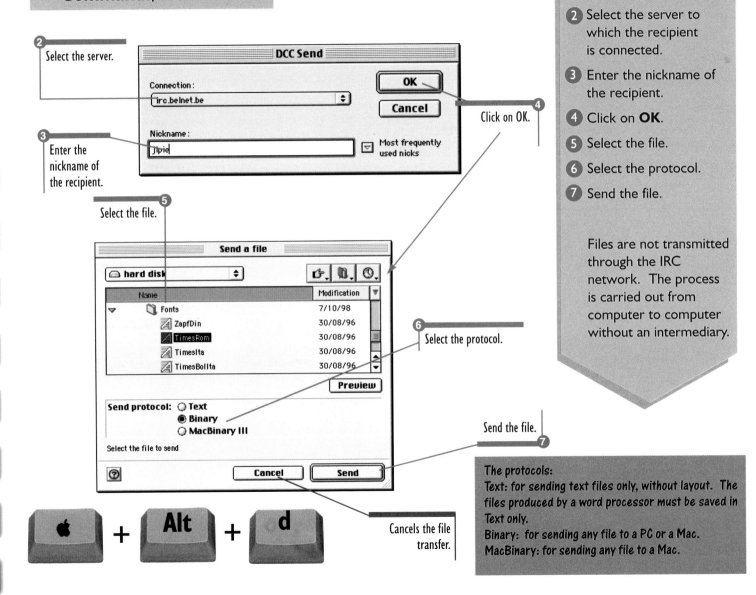

Select the server.

DCC Send

Connection:
irc.belnet.be

OK

Cancel

Click on OK.

Nickname:
Jlpie

Most frequently used nicks

Select the file.

Send a file

hard disk

Name	Modification
▽ Fonts	7/10/98
ZapfDin	30/08/96
TimesRom	30/08/96
TimesIta	30/08/96
TimesBolIta	30/08/96

Preview

Send protocol: ○ Text
● Binary
○ MacBinary III

Select the file to send

Select the protocol.

Send the file.

Cancel   Send

Cancels the file transfer.

＋ Alt ＋ d

The DCC status window

DCC Chat

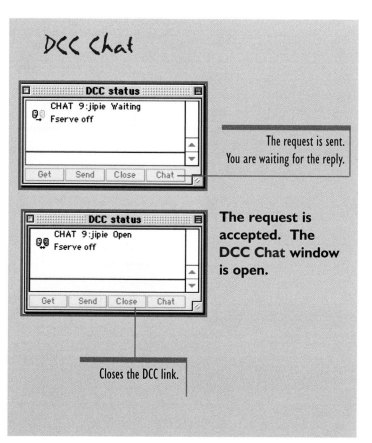

The request is sent. You are waiting for the reply.

The request is accepted. The DCC Chat window is open.

Closes the DCC link.

Send DCC files

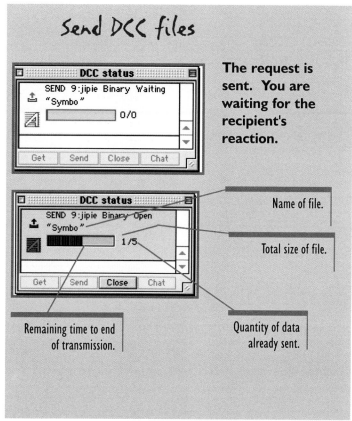

The request is sent. You are waiting for the recipient's reaction.

Name of file.

Total size of file.

Remaining time to end of transmission.

Quantity of data already sent.

The messages

.... you receive ....

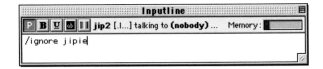

Public standard message.
Action message sent by jopp with the /me command.
Message from the server: you have been sent a CTC Ping command.
Message from the server: jip is leaving the #marabout channel.

If one of the participants is too noisy, vulgar, aggressive, or annoying, you can prevent his or her messages from being displayed. Select the Commands/Ignore command. Enter the nickname of the user to be ignored.

In the Console window

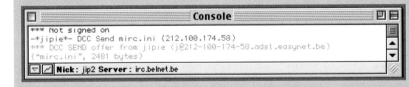

You have changed your i mode.
Message from the server: you are invited to join the #marabout channel.
Private message from jopp. You can reply with a private message (Commands/Message) or by opening a Query window (Commands/Query).

You are not informed if somebody requests information about you (Whois).

Receive a DCC chat request

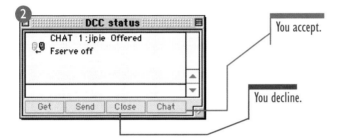

You accept.

You decline.

Checklist

1 jipie requests a DCC chat.

2 You open the DCC Status window (in the Windows menu).

Receive a DCC file

You accept.

You decline.

Checklist

1 jipie offers you a file.

2 You open the DCC Status window (in the Windows menu).

Accept only files whose contents you know and which come from reliable users.

You are the operator

Yes, you can be the operator (the boss) of a channel. All you have to do is join a channel whose name does not yet exist on the server. You automatically become the channel operator: your nickname is preceded by the @ sign in the right pane of the channel window.

As a channel operator, you can change the operating mode of the channel, kick, op or deop a user, and so on.

The channel will close automatically and disappear as soon as the last user has left – it is not permanent. You must create it again every time you connect.

TIP

Click on the Topic field at the bottom of the channel window and enter the topic of the channel.

Activate the t (topic) mode of the channel to prevent visitors from changing the topic.

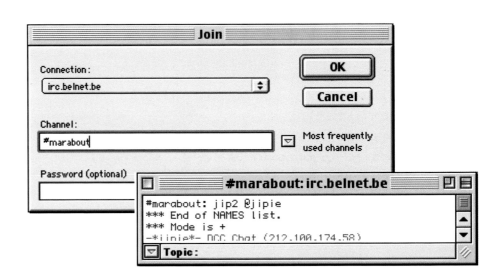

Join

Connection:
irc.belnet.be

OK

Cancel

Channel:
#marabout

Most frequently used channels

Password (optional)

#marabout: irc.belnet.be

#marabout: jip2 @jipie
*** End of NAMES list.
*** Mode is +
-*jipie*- DCC Chat (212.100.174.58)

Topic :

Windows/Users

Windows/Users

Notes

The Participants window contains the commands for the participants and the modes of the channel.

When a user gets operator status, he/she has access to all the commands reserved for operators.

Hint
See description of modes on page 17.

jip2 is the operator because his nickname is in red.

Modes of the channel. Drag the small cursor to activate a mode.

Ops the selected participant.

Deops the selected participant.

Kicks out the selected participant.

Bans the selected participant.

Kicks out and bans the selected participant.

Full identification of the user who will be banned.

Users with this name will be banned.

Users with this nickname will be banned.

Users connecting from this computer will be banned.

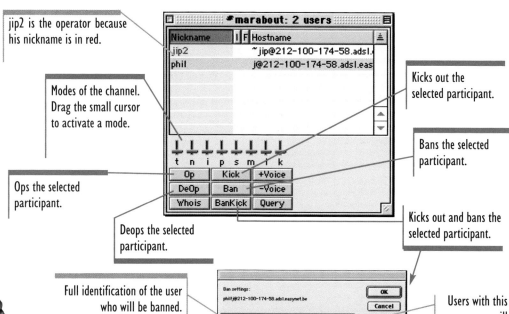

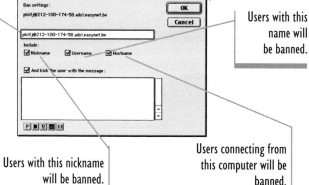

Mode

t	Only an operator can change the topic.
n	Messages from the outside will be ignored.
i	Users join by invitation only.
p	Private channel.
s	Secret channel.
m	Moderated channel.
l	Maximum number of participants.
k	A password is required to join the channel.

Personalise the users window

File/Preferences (Buttons tab)

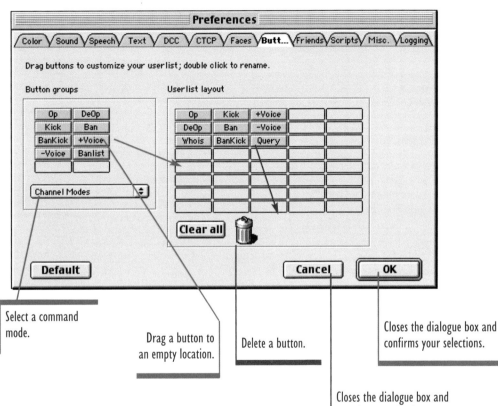

Notes

Select the File/Preferences command.

The IRCle will have many personalisation settings: in particular, additional buttons can be inserted in the **Users** window to complete the commands.

Explore the other preference tabs yourself. The settings are clearly defined.

Select a command mode.

Drag a button to an empty location.

Delete a button.

Closes the dialogue box and confirms your selections.

Closes the dialogue box and cancels your selections.

The Banlist button is indispensable. It opens the list of banned users so that you can edit it.

PART II:

Direct communication

Direct communication

The principle of direct communication software is very simple. A set of inter-connected servers links all the users connected to them. When you connect to one of these servers you are identified and can communicate instantly and directly with all the other users.

This network of servers plays several roles: it informs the other users of your presence on the Internet, links users for a private or collective chat and makes it possible to send messages that will be transmitted directly to the recipient without having to go via their mailboxes. These software applications are interesting for users who log on from time to time and for those who are connected permanently. In an Intranet network, they facilitate the communication and rapid transmission of information.

The simplest direct communication software is limited to the pager function: sending and receiving short messages. In certain cases, the messages may even be sent over the telephone. This is useful for sending a brief message to a 'surfaholic' who ties up his or her line for long hours.

Unlike IRC, there is no inter-connection between the different networks. For example, the users of the ICQ network unfortunately cannot communicate with those of the PowWow network.

Software

ICQ

ICQ is the most famous of all direct communication programs. Its logo is an integral part of the Internet landscape. The Israeli publishers Mirabilis, proud (and rightly so) of their success, boast several million subscribers. Each of them has a **Universal Internet Number**, or **UIN**, which is appearing more and more frequently on business cards and at the bottom of e-mail messages.

There are many versions, depending on the operating system: : **Mac 68 K, PowerMac, BeOS, Windows 3.x, Windows 95/98/2000/NT4, Windows CE** and even **PalmPilot**.

This book will deal in detail with the version for Windows 95/98 (the most complete). See page 103.
A shorter section is devoted to the Macintosh version. See page 161.

PowWow

Publisher: Tribal Voice
Publisher's website: http://www.tribal.com
Download from:
http://ww2.tribal.com/download/default.cfm
System requirements: Windows 95, 98, NT4, 2000, OS/2, PowerMac, Unix
Very similar to **ICQ**, it offers some special features, such as voice reading of messages, automatic answering device and photo display of your contacts.

AOL Instant Messenger

Publisher: AOL
Publisher's website: http://www.aol.com
Download from: http://www.aol.com/aim
System requirements: Windows 95, 98, NT4, 2000, CE, Mac
AOL Instant Messenger enables you to stay in contact with a list of other users to send them short messages and to chat. You can also subscribe to a newsletter server in fields that interest you.

Yahoo Messenger

Publisher : Yahoo !
Publisher's website : http://www.yahoo.com
Download from:
http://messenger.yahoo.com
System requirements: Windows 95, 98, NT4 or 2000, Mac, Unix, PalmOS
In addition to its famous directory, Yahoo! offers a free direct communication program. It displays the contact list on line and allows you to send short messages and communicate directly with voice chat. It also offers an agenda (with reminder) and consults your Yahoo! mailbox.

MSN Messenger Service

Messenger Service

Publisher : Microsoft
Publisher's website : http://www.microsoft.com
Download from:
http://messenger.msn.com
System requirements: Windows 95, 98, NT4 or 2000, MacOS from version 8.0 (with Internet Explorer from version 3)
Microsoft offers its instant communication software that informs you when your friends are online so you can talk to them on the Internet. Access to your Hotmail is made easier. You can even see from Outlook Express whether your friends are on line. Search by keywords.

Chapter 3

ICQ for Windows

Introducing ICQ for Windows

When you spell **ICQ** out loud, you hear 'I seek you'. The very first rule of **ICQ** is actually to answer the question: 'Is such and such a user currently connected to the Internet?' For the **ICQ** to be able to find him or her, the user in question must obviously be an **ICQ** subscriber and connected to one of the **ICQ** servers. A direct communication can then be established with each of the users on line for a private (DCC) chat, to send files and so on.

Publisher: Mirabilis (http://www.mirabilis.com) - ICQ website: http://www.icq.com
Shareware
System requirements: Windows 95, 98, NT4, 2000 or 3.x

Download from: http://www.icq.com/download/step-by-step.html (for Windows 95/98/NT4/2000) - 5 Mb
http://www.icq.com/download/step-by-step-31x.html (for Windows 3.x) - 1,3 Mb

Two good addresses:
- http://hol.freethemes.com/insideicq.htm
- http://www.cnet.com/Content/Reports/Special/ICQ/index.html

The News server installed by Mirabilis is public (news.mirabilis.com).
See these forums: alt.chat.icq, icq.chat, icq.public.pc.tech.

> ### TIP
> What can you do with the ICQ ?
>
> Be informed when another ICQ subscriber logs on to the Internet.
>
> Inform other users that you are on the Internet.
>
> Send to and receive quick messages from ICQ users.
>
> Receive express messages from non ICQ users.
>
> Send and receive files.
>
> Send and receive website addresses.
>
> Chat directly and in private.
>
> Check periodically for the arrival of messages in your e-mail box.
>
> Use certain security measures so as not to be disturbed.

Connecting for the first time

Install the program by clicking twice on the icon of the file you have downloaded. You can then register as an ICQ user. You must log on to the Internet first because the ICQ server attributes your subscriber number (ICQ #) directly.

In the event of a fatal error during the installation, start Windows again and close all open applications before beginning the installation again. If you are using Windows 3.x and you receive an error message relating to the comctl32.dll file, install the Win32s version obtainable from this address:
http://www.icq.com/pub/win31/pw1118s.exe

Your personal details will be registered in the ICQ user directory. Complete only what you consider useful for the public to know. You can change your personal details at any time (see page 130).

(see page 130).

HOW TO
Change your personal details: click on the ICQ button and select Add-Change current user/View-Change my details.

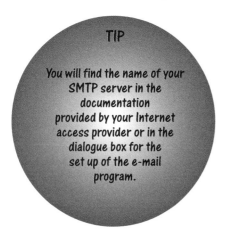

TIP

You will find the name of your SMTP server in the documentation provided by your Internet access provider or in the dialogue box for the set up of the e-mail program.

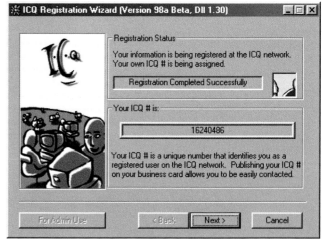

ICQ Registration Wizard (Version 98a Beta, DII 1.30)

Registration Status
Your information is being registered at the ICQ network. Your own ICQ # is being assigned.

Registration Completed Successfully

Your ICQ # is:
16240486

Your ICQ # is a unique number that identifies you as a registered user on the ICQ network. Publishing your ICQ # on your business card allows you to be easily contacted.

For Admin Use   < Back   Next >   Cancel

The registration steps

Click on Next to go to the next step of your registration.

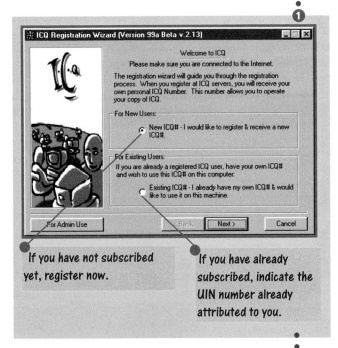

1

If you have not subscribed yet, register now.

If you have already subscribed, indicate the UIN number already attributed to you.

2

You are connected via a modem.

You are connected to the Internet via a local area network or a cable/ADSL modem.

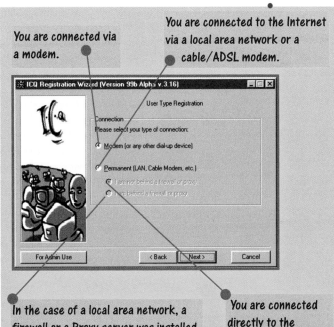

In the case of a local area network, a firewall or a Proxy server was installed by the network administrator. Ask the network administrator.

You are connected directly to the Internet, without an intermediary (which is generally the case when you have a cable modem).

The registration
...... steps (cont.) ......

3

Enter your e-mail address.

Enter the nickname by which you wish to be known to the ICQ server and the other users.

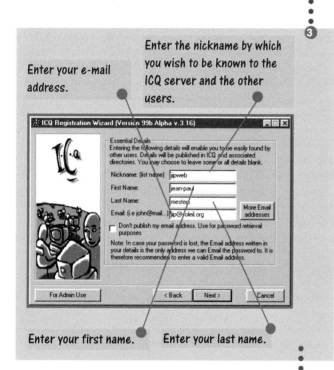

Enter your first name.

Enter your last name.

You may refrain from completing this dialogue box to preserve your anonymity to some extent.

You do not wish to be included in the Mirabilis statistics.

Select your type of occupation and place where you use the ICQ (at work or at home).

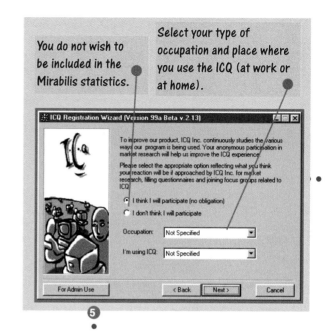

5

Enter any additional details.

Enter your details.

4

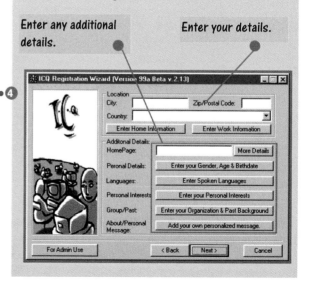

Enter a password.

Enter your password again (to confirm it).

Activate this option so that you do not have to enter your password every time you start ICQ to connect to the server.

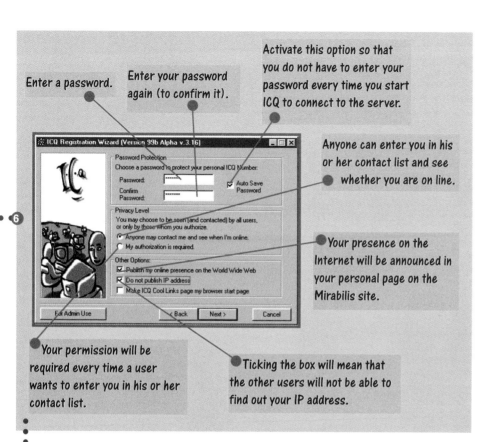

Anyone can enter you in his or her contact list and see whether you are on line.

Your presence on the Internet will be announced in your personal page on the Mirabilis site.

Your permission will be required every time a user wants to enter you in his or her contact list.

Ticking the box will mean that the other users will not be able to find out your IP address.

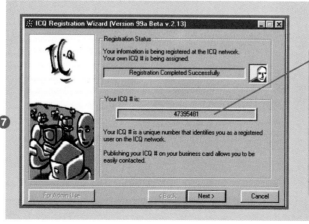

The ICQ server attributes an ICQ number to you. You are henceforth a member of the big, happy ICQ family.

The registration
...... steps (cont.) ....

8

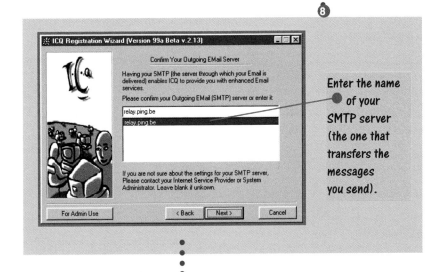

Enter the name of your SMTP server (the one that transfers the messages you send).

ICQ suggests that you add users(see page 114).

9

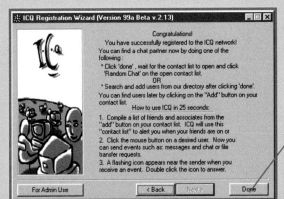

Click here to end your registration.

The ICQ window

The installation program creates a folder in the Start window called Mirabilis **ICQ**, which contains, in particular, the Launch **ICQ** command. **ICQ** opens automatically every time you start Windows but remains inactive as long as you have not connected to the Internet.

At the far right of the Windows taskbar, the **ICQ** flower is red when the **ICQ** server is not detected and green when you are connected to the **ICQ** network.

HOW TO
You can cancel the automatic ICQ launch. Click on the Menu button and select Preferences. Click on the Connection tab and cancel the Launch ICQ on startup.

 off line

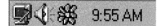 on line

Open the ICQ window by clicking twice on the flower in the taskbar.

TIP

If you cannot manage to connect (the flower remains stubbornly red), it is probably because of a failure in the ICQ network.

Just try again.

The ICQ window

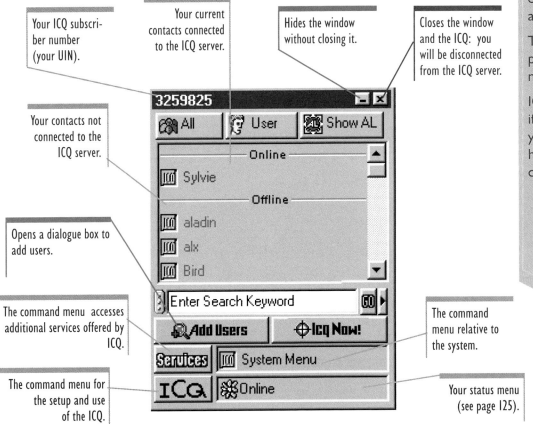

Your ICQ subscriber number (your UIN).

Your current contacts connected to the ICQ server.

Hides the window without closing it.

Closes the window and the ICQ: you will be disconnected from the ICQ server.

Your contacts not connected to the ICQ server.

Opens a dialogue box to add users.

The command menu accesses additional services offered by ICQ.

The command menu for the setup and use of the ICQ.

The command menu relative to the system.

Your status menu (see page 125).

Notes

To display the ICQ window, double click on the flower in the Windows taskbar or click with the right button and select **Open ICQ.**

The **ICQ Now!** button is present only if the advanced mode is active.

ICQ continues to run even if its window is hidden. If you close the window, however, you close your connection to ICQ.

How is the ICQ window integrated in the Windows environment? Click on the ICQ button and select Windows/Alert.

Always On Top : the ICQ window remains in the foreground at all times, on top of all the other windows.

Auto Minimize : the ICQ window will be automatically hidden after remaining open for a few seconds.

Notes

ICQ offers two menu modes: the simple mode containing the most common commands, and the advanced mode which gives access to all the commands. At the bottom of the field for friends and associates, click on the To Simple Mode or To Advanced Mode button.

The menu attached to each user and the system menu are opened by clicking either on the right or on the left mouse button. If you click with an inappropriate button, a dialogue box will suggest that you activate one or the other button.

The menus and the mouse

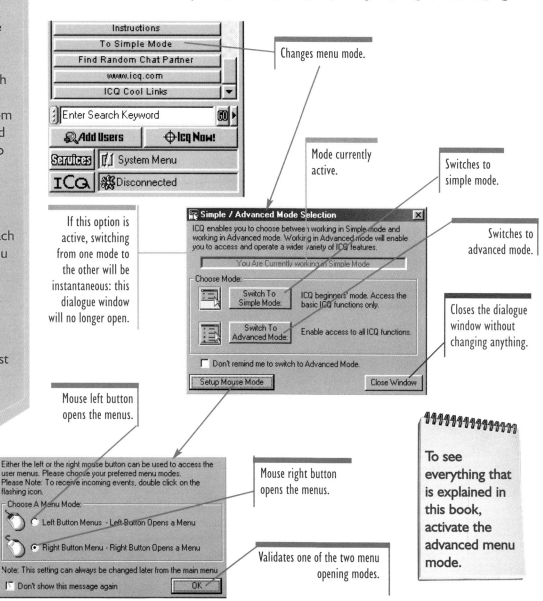

Changes menu mode.

Mode currently active.

Switches to simple mode.

Switches to advanced mode.

If this option is active, switching from one mode to the other will be instantaneous: this dialogue window will no longer open.

Closes the dialogue window without changing anything.

Mouse left button opens the menus.

Mouse right button opens the menus.

If this option is active, the dialogue box will no longer open in the future.

Validates one of the two menu opening modes.

To see everything that is explained in this book, activate the advanced menu mode.

Add users to your contact list

Add Users button

Without a contact list, the **ICQ** is virtually paralysed. You must therefore create a list of persons with whom you wish to correspond. As soon as one member from this list connects to the **ICQ** server, you are informed by a sound and that person's name goes from the offline to the online field.

To add a user to your list, you need the user's name, e-mail address and still, if possible, his or her **ICQ** number.

HOW TO

In the Search Result window, the last column of the table, called Authorize, indicates either Authorize (the user will agree or decline to be included in your contact list), or Always (user authorisation is not required). This setting is defined by the user him/herself.

TIP

You will find lists of users at the following addresses:

http://www.cc.umist.ac.uk/~mikec/icq/icq.htm

http://www.mirageworks.com/icqcanada

http://www.icq.com/people

http://groups.icq.com

Find a contact

Add Users button

Enter the information in one of the three fields.

Enter the full e-mail address (e.g.: phil@uk.net).

Close the dialogue window without carrying out a search.

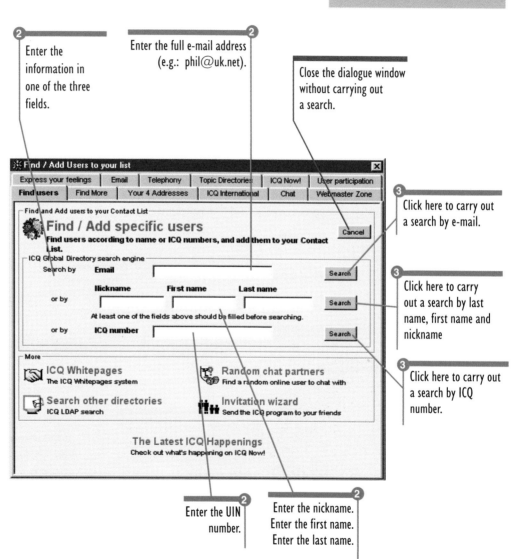

Click here to carry out a search by e-mail.

Click here to carry out a search by last name, first name and nickname

Click here to carry out a search by ICQ number.

Enter the UIN number.

Enter the nickname.
Enter the first name.
Enter the last name.

Your search is unsuccessful

Add Users button

Enter e-mail address of the user you are searching for.

Enter e-mail address of the user to whom you want to send a message.

Sends prepared message to invite a user to use ICQ, accompanied by any text you may have added.

ICQ Global Directory Search Engine

Email | Details | ICQ #

Enter the user's valid Email address:

Search Users By Email

EMail: jiiiip@ping.ne

Search Again
Stop Search
New Search
Wizard Mode

Unable to Locate User(s)
You can execute any of the following commands on a user's
Email address:

jiiiip@ping.ne   Send Email   Preview Letter

Search In Other Directory Services

☑ Invite your friend to join ICQ by emailing to the above address an invitation form letter from you.

Add a personalized message to him/her about ICQ.

☑ Notify me when he/she registers on the ICQ network.
☑ Automatically add me to the user's contact list when he logs on.

Add a personalised message via e-mail inviting the user to use ICQ.

Sends form letter with your personalised message.

Shows preview of the message that will be sent.

Note

If the user you are looking for was not found, it is not necessarily because s/he does not exist. You may have made a typing error in the information you provided or the user in question may not be an ICQ subscriber.

Preview

Greetings,

I have tried to contact you on the ICQ network but was unable to find
Therefore I would like to invite you to join the ICQ Network. You can d
Once you do it, we will be able to communicate on-line.

Click here to download ICQ:

http://www.icq.com/

How to find me on the ICQ Network:

I have 4 addresses on the ICQ Network:
- My ICQ number is 3259825
- My Personal Communication Center on the Web, from which you can

OK

When the user identified by e-mail connects to an ICQ server, he/she will immediately receive a request from you to be added to his/her contact list.

The user identified by e-mail is entered in your waiting contact list. You will be informed when s/he is registered as an ICQ user.

Notes

If your search is by an e-mail address or UIN number, the list will be limited to a single user.

If your search criterion is not very precise, the list will be too long and the ICQ server will ask you to narrow down your search by providing more details.

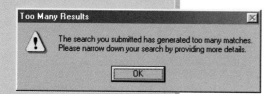

Too Many Results

⚠ The search you submitted has generated too many matches. Please narrow down your search by providing more details.

[OK]

The message is not sent to the user's mailbox but transferred directly through the ICQ server. If the user is connected to ICQ, the message will reach him/her directly. Otherwise, it will remain waiting until the next time that user connects.
See page 140.

Your search is successful

Add Users button

You can search by: e-mail, ICQ number, last name, first name or nickname of the contact you are searching for.

ICQ Global Directory Search Engine

| Email | Details | ICQ # |

Search Again
Stop Search
New Search
Wizard Mode

Search Users By Parameters

Nickname: phil
First Name:
Last Name:

Drag here to widen the column.

Found 40 User(s). Double click on a user in order to add him/her

ICQ #	Nick Na...	First	Last	Email	Authorize
100874 Phil		Philippe	Artsztein	philippe...	Always
102682 Phil					Authorize
104518 phil		philip	swamidoss	S..Swam...	Always
112024 Phil		Philip	Pelanne	phil@ne...	Authorize
113413 Phil		Phil		pwb@so...	Authorize
121213 Phil		phil		talltree@...	Authorize
122945 phil		Phil		philipt@...	Authorize
123807 Phil				philfer@...	Always
124168 Phil		Phil	Krzywicki	barfboy...	Always
125069 Phil		Philip	T.	ptys@ne...	Always
127348 phil		philip	hoffman	phoffma...	Always

Click twice on a name to add the contact to your list or to send him/her an authorisation request to add him/her to the list.

The user list corresponding to your search criteria.

Flow chart of a request to add a contact to your list

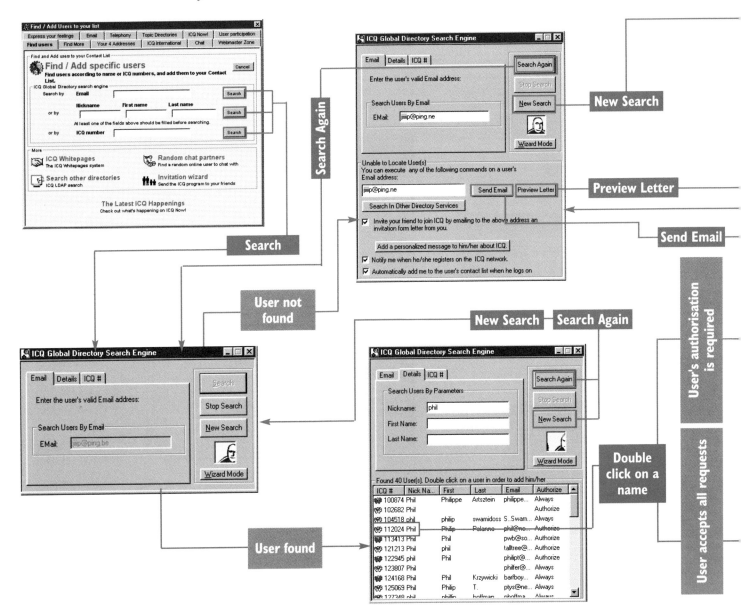

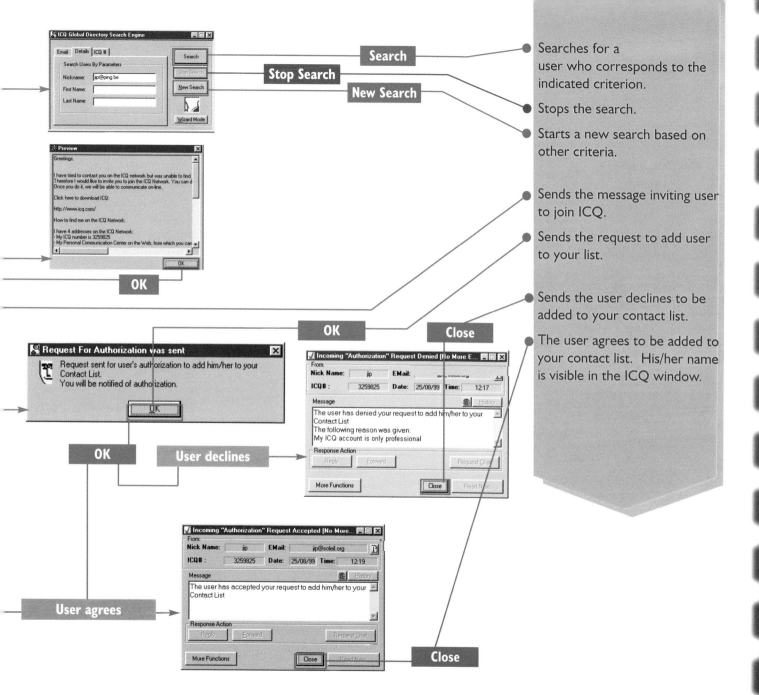

Searches for a user who corresponds to the indicated criterion.

Stops the search.

Starts a new search based on other criteria.

Sends the message inviting user to join ICQ.

Sends the request to add user to your list.

Sends the user declines to be added to your contact list.

The user agrees to be added to your contact list. His/her name is visible in the ICQ window.

Your request for authorisation to add user

Add Users button

Your request is sent directly to the user who will receive it as soon as s/he is connected to an ICQ server.

Indicate why you want to add this user to your contact list.

Message confirming that your request was sent.

Click here to close the message.

The user declines to be added to your list.

The user agrees to be added to your list.

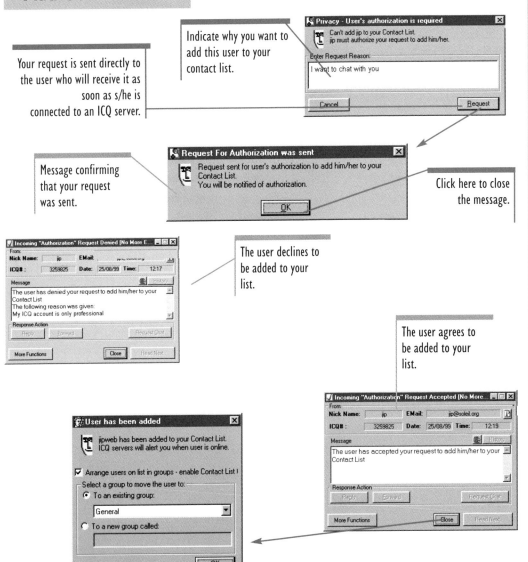

Notes

When wish to add a user to your list, click on the Add Users button.

If the user wishes to give his or her authorisation to be added to the list, ICQ opens a message window directly. The user who receives the request agrees or declines to be added to your list.

While waiting for the authorisation of a user to be added to your contact list, his/her name is in a waiting list called Awaiting authorization in your ICQ window.

Your contacts

Your contact list will extend gradually and may grow to a considerable size. The ICQ window will soon become too small to display them all.

Fortunately, you can group your contacts by categories; furthermore, ICQ enters each user automatically in an address book where all their details are stored. When you click on the name of a user in the contact list, you open a menu containing all the commands relative to that user.

To find out who is online, simply open the ICQ window and consult the Online field. However, it is much better to be informed immediately (by sound or on screen) as soon as one of your contacts logs on. In the ICQ window, click the name of a contact and select More (Rename, Delete, ...)/Alert-Accept Mode. Now, click on the Alert tab, and select Enable Online Alert.

TIP

Information about the users comes from the server. It is supplied by the user him/herself. Although there is no reason to doubt its authenticity, there is no reason either to accept it with full confidence.

HOW TO
Display your more important contacts by having them float outside the ICQ window. In the user menu, select More/Floating On. The labels of the floating users will always be in the foreground in relation to the other windows.

Your contact list

User/Groups button

Opens and closes the group.

Switches the display of groups on / off.

Sends an ICQ message to a group member or to the entire group (see page 140).

Sends an Internet address to a group member or to the entire group (see page 153).

Sends an e-mail to a group member or to the entire group (see page 143).

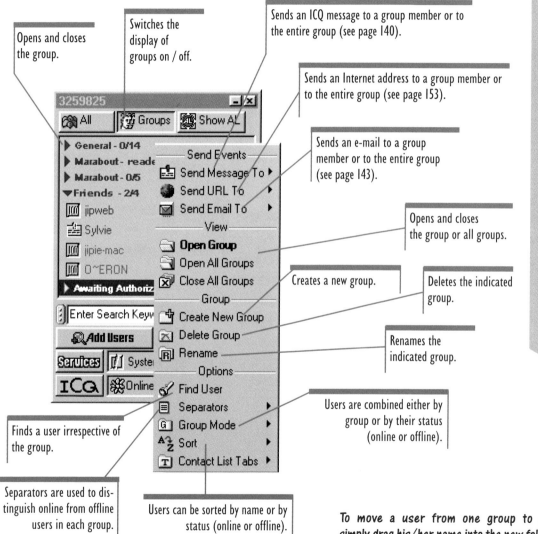

Opens and closes the group or all groups.

Creates a new group.

Deletes the indicated group.

Renames the indicated group.

Users are combined either by group or by their status (online or offline).

Finds a user irrespective of the group.

Separators are used to distinguish online from offline users in each group.

Users can be sorted by name or by status (online or offline).

Notes

When you click on the All/Online button, you display either all the contacts, or only those who are online.

When you click on the User/Groups button, you display the contacts either as a long list or grouped by categories.

To access the group management commands, click with the right mouse button on the User/Groups button or click on the name of a group.

To move a user from one group to another, simply drag his/her name into the new folder.

Notes

Click on the Menu button and select the Address Book command.

Click with the right mouse button on the name of a user to open the menu with the command pertaining to that user.

Your address book

ICQ/Address Book

Select the user whose details you wish to consult.

Click on the other tabs to view the other information.

Add an additional address for the user.

Send an e-mail.

Rename the user.

Delete the user.

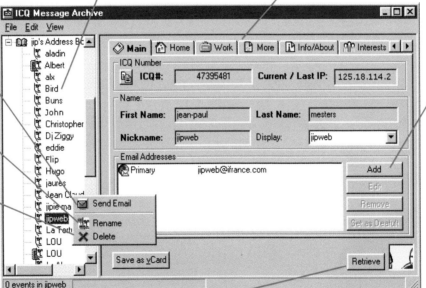

When you remove a user from the ICQ window, a message suggests that you remove that user from the address book too.

ICQ server updates the information concerning the selected user.

Click on the name of a user in the ICQ window, then click on More to obtain the Rename and Delete commands.

Your presence online

When you are connected to one of the **ICQ** servers, you are, in principle, visible and can be contacted by subscribers who have your name in their contact list. In reality, you are free to choose a status: 'Do not disturb', 'Away' or 'Privacy' for all the users or for certain users only.

Furthermore, when another subscriber wants to add you to his/her contact list, you may request that it is not done without your authorisation.

Your ICQ subscription does not preclude you from taking other security measures (for example : it does not hide your **IP** address). While remaining available to other users, you can take certain precautions that will shelter you from unwelcome intruders. See page 157.

HOW TO
Each ICQ user has a personal page on the ICQ site. His/her address is: http://wwp.mirabilis.com/ICQ# Replace ICQ# by the user's number, e.g.: http://wwp.mirabilis.com/3259825

TIP
Activate the Away status automatically if you are going to be away from your PC or when the screen saver is displayed. Your contacts will no longer try vainly to correspond with you, thinking that you are still at your computer.

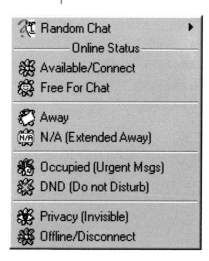

Note

The Offline/Disconnect status is automatically activated when you disconnect from the Internet. The status you had when you disconnected will be automatically reactivated next time you connect.

Your status

Available/Connect	You are online and everybody can contact you.
Free for chat	You are available for a chat in real time. See page 146 for details.
Away	You are away from your keyboard for a short period. You are therefore not available, but are still online. Users who try to contact you will receive the message you have prepared. The messages they sent to you will be waiting until you return.
N/A (Extended Away)	You are away from your keyboard for an extended period, but you remain online. This status is very similar to **Away**.
Occupied (Urgent Msgs)	You are occupied and you do not wish to be disturbed unnecessarily. The message you have prepared will be sent to the users who try to contact you. You will be notified only if urgent messages come in. The other messages will remain waiting until you are available again.
DND (Do not Disturb)	You are very busy and do not wish to be disturbed at all, not even for urgent messages. All messages will remain waiting.
Privacy (Invisible)	The other users see your name in their **Offline** list, although you are still online.
Offline/Disconnected	You have disconnected from the **ICQ** server.

Select your status

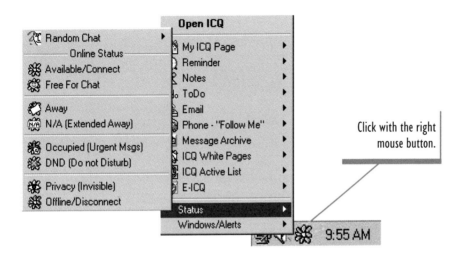

Click with the right mouse button.

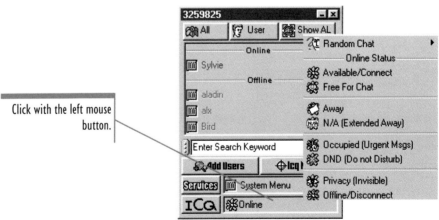

Click with the left mouse button.

When you click with the right mouse button on the ICQ icon or on the Services button, you access a Reminder, a notepad (Notes) and a ToDo list. ICQ must be open for Reminder to display the programmed reminders.

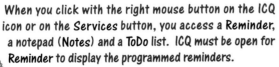

Status message creation flow chart

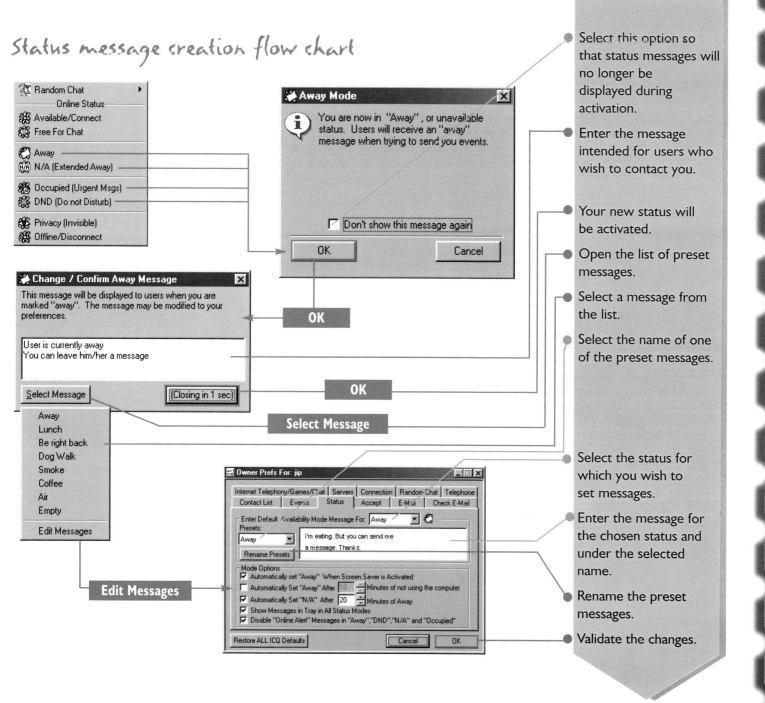

- Select this option so that status messages will no longer be displayed during activation.

- Enter the message intended for users who wish to contact you.

- Your new status will be activated.

- Open the list of preset messages.

- Select a message from the list.

- Select the name of one of the preset messages.

- Select the status for which you wish to set messages.

- Enter the message for the chosen status and under the selected name.

- Rename the preset messages.

- Validate the changes.

Status settings

ICQ/Preferences & Security/Preferences(Status tab)

The Away status will be set automatically as soon as the Windows screen saver is activated.

The Away status will be set x minutes after the computer was last used.

The N/A status will be set automatically if the Away status is active for x minutes.

Click to restore the default values for all the ICQ settings.

The connection notifications of one of your contacts will not be displayed when your status is Away, Occupied, DND or A/N.

If you receive messages, the ICQ log in the taskbar will be replaced by a 'message logo' irrespective of which status is active.

Closes the dialogue box and activates the options as set.

Closes the dialogue box without saving the changes you have made to the options.

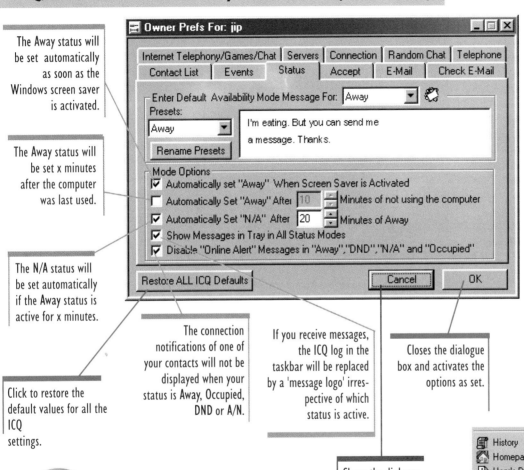

Owner Prefs For: jip

Internet Telephony/Games/Chat | Servers | Connection | Random Chat | Telephone
Contact List | Events | Status | Accept | E-Mail | Check E-Mail

Enter Default Availability Mode Message For: Away

Presets:
Away

Rename Presets

I'm eating. But you can send me a message. Thanks.

Mode Options
- ☑ Automatically set "Away" When Screen Saver is Activated
- ☐ Automatically Set "Away" After 10 Minutes of not using the computer
- ☑ Automatically Set "N/A" After 20 Minutes of Away
- ☑ Show Messages in Tray in All Status Modes
- ☑ Disable "Online Alert" Messages in "Away","DND","N/A" and "Occupied"

Restore ALL ICQ Defaults | Cancel | OK

The status you choose for a specific user is active for this user irrespective of which general status is active

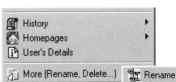

History ▶
Homepages ▶
User's Details

More (Rename, Delete...) | Rename
X Delete
Alert/Accept Modes
"Floating" On

Notes

Click on the ICQ button and select Preferences & Security/Preferences. Click on the Status tab.

Irrespective of your general status, you can set a specific status for a specific user. You can, for example, take the general status DND but remain available for a specific user. Click on the name of the user concerned and select the **More/Alert/Accept Modes** command. Validate the **Online Status** option and validate the option corresponding to the status you wish to activate.

Notes

Click on the ICQ button and select Preferences & Security/Security & Privacy.

Complete the three lists (Ignore List, Invisible List and Visible List) with the names of the users for whom you wish to: ignore all chat requests (Ignore List); remain invisible at all times (Invisible list); or remain visible at all times(Visible List) irrespective of your status.

Your security

ICQ/Preferences & Security/Security & Privacy

All users who want to add you to their contact list can do so without requesting your authorisation.

Your authorisation is required before a user can add you to his/her contact list.

Enter the new password.

Security (Ignore/Spam, harrasment control) For: jip

Security | Ignore List | Invisible List | Visible List

Change Contact List Authorization:
- ○ All users may add me to their contact list
- ● My authorization is required

IP Hiding:
- ☑ Do not allow others to see my IP address

Change Password:
- New Password:
- Retype New Password:
- ☑ Save Password

Web Aware:
- ☑ Allow others to view my online presence on the World Wide Web

Security Level
- ● Low — Password will automatically be saved and used
- ○ Medium — Password must be entered to change user information only
- ○ High — Password must be entered to load ICQ

More About ICQ Security (Web Guide) | Cancel | Save

Enter the new password a second time (to confirm it).

Your password is automatically saved and will be used each time as needed without your having to enter it again.

Tick this option so that your IP address does not appear in information about you (in the address book of other users).

If this option is ticked, your presence online will be visible to all users on your personal page, irrespective of your status.

Closes the dialogue box.

Saves the settings on the ICQ server.

Security levels
Low	If this option is active you will not have to enter the password next time you start ICQ.
Medium	The password will be required if you wish to change your details on the ICQ server.
High	The password will be required every time you start ICQ.

If you have lost your password, connect to the Mirabilis site at http://www.icq.com/password to request a new password.

Your personal details

ICQ/Add-Change current user/View-Change my Details

Checklist

1 Click on the ICQ button, select Add/Change current User and then View/Change my Details.

2 Change your details in the tabs.

3 Save your details on the ICQ server.

Change your details in the four tabs of this dialogue box.

If this option is active, your e-mail address will not be published. It will however be useful to retrieve your password if you should forget it.

Deletes your details from the ICQ directory.

Retrieves your details as saved on the ICQ server.

Closes the dialogue box without saving anything.

Save your details on the ICQ server.

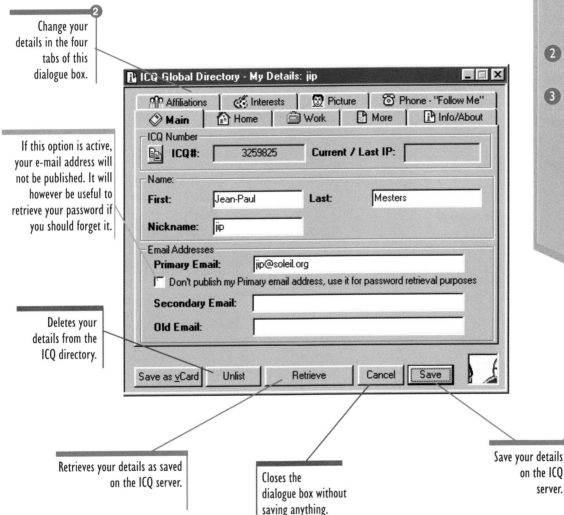

ICQ Global Directory - My Details: jip

Affiliations | Interests | Picture | Phone - "Follow Me"
Main | Home | Work | More | Info/About

ICQ Number
ICQ#: 3259825   Current / Last IP:

Name:
First: Jean-Paul   Last: Mesters
Nickname: jip

Email Addresses
Primary Email: jip@soleil.org
☐ Don't publish my Primary email address, use it for password retrieval purposes
Secondary Email:
Old Email:

Save as vCard | Unlist | Retrieve | Cancel | Save

Notes

What happens when a user wishes to add you to his/her contact list? The ICQ icon is replaced by a blinking icon. Click on it twice. If you have imposed no restriction, you will be informed without further ado. If your authorisation is required (see page 129), you can accept or refuse.

If you accept, you will receive a message as soon as you are added to the other user's contact list.

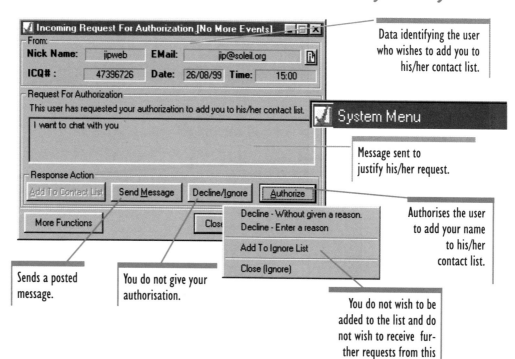

Data identifying the user who wishes to add you to his/her contact list.

System Menu

Message sent to justify his/her request.

Authorises the user to add your name to his/her contact list.

Sends a posted message.

You do not give your authorisation.

You do not wish to be added to the list and do not wish to receive further requests from this user.

You are added to the contact list of this user.

Opens the dialogue box on information concerning this user.

System Menu

Adds this user to your own contact list.

Your mailbox

Check New E-mail

You can ask **ICQ** to play the role of watchdog, informing you when new e-mail has arrived in your mailbox. To do this, you must provide all of your e-mail settings: the name of the **POP3** server (the server that keeps e-mail for you), your logon (name by which you are known by the e-mail) and your password. You will find these data on the documents sent by your access provider or in the dialogue box for setting your e-mail software.

Warning: the messages you receive in your mailbox are completely independent of those you receive directly through ICQ. There is no danger of confusing the two.

HOW TO

Your e-mail is checked automatically on a regular basis, but you can also check immediately with the Email/Check New Email command from the Services menu, or from the ICQ log in the Windows taskbar.

TIP

It makes no sense to check your mailbox every other minute. Every 10 to 15 minutes will do.

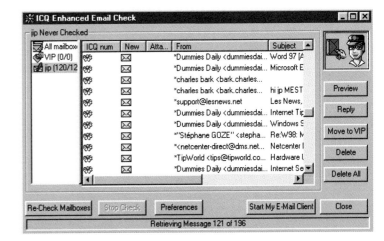

Notes

Click on the ICQ button and select Preferences & Security/Email Preferences.

Click on the Accounts tab to enter the settings of your mailboxes and on the Email Client tab to indicate the e-mail software you are using.

Warning

The e-mail password you are using may be different from the one that gives you access to the Internet. Check the documentation of your access provider.

Set e-mail retrieval

ICQ/Preferences & Security/Email Preferences

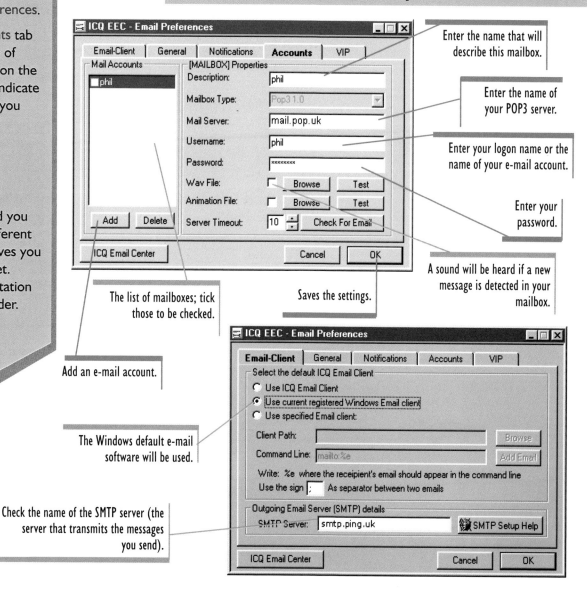

Enter the name that will describe this mailbox.

Enter the name of your POP3 server.

Enter your logon name or the name of your e-mail account.

Enter your password.

A sound will be heard if a new message is detected in your mailbox.

The list of mailboxes; tick those to be checked.

Saves the settings.

Add an e-mail account.

The Windows default e-mail software will be used.

Check the name of the SMTP server (the server that transmits the messages you send).

Set e-mail retrieval

ICQ/Preferences & Security/Email Preferences

Tick this option to show only new e-mails.

Tick this option for periodic checking of your mailbox.

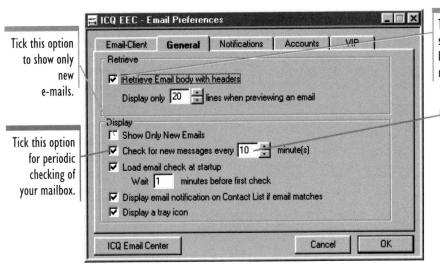

Tick this option to see the body and headers of the messages.

Enter the time (in minutes) between two checks.

If you wish to be informed visually about new messages, select the notification mode.

A dialogue box will open.

A sound will alert you.

Select the sound.

If you wish to be alerted by a sound signal when new e-mail comes in, select the notification mode.

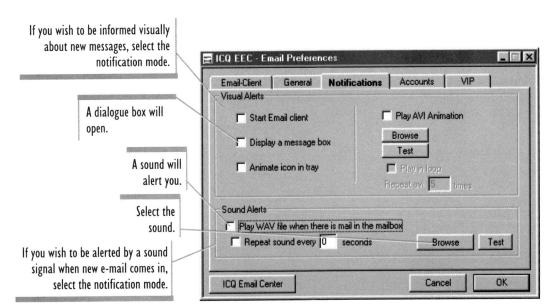

Notes

Click on the ICQ button and select Preferences & Security/ Email Preferences.

Click on the General tab to enter the check settings of your mailboxes and on the Notifications tab to indicate how you wish to be informed about new incoming mail.

To avoid overloading the server, the interval between two checks of your mailbox should be greater than 10 minutes.

Notes

Every time that ICQ checks your mailbox, it informs you accordingly if you have ticked this option (see preceding page).

If you have requested the retrieval of the headers, ICQ displays them in a dialogue box.

You have new mail

Email/Check New Email

In this window, delete the messages you do not wish to download in your e-mail program. They will be deleted directly on the e-mail server.

Drag the border between two column labels to change their width.

Sender.

Subject of the e-mails.

Previews the contents of the selected e-mail.

Click here to reply to the selected e-mail.

Deletes the selected e-mail from your mailbox.

Opens your e-mail program.

The number of e-mails in your mailbox and the number of e-mails retrieved in this window.

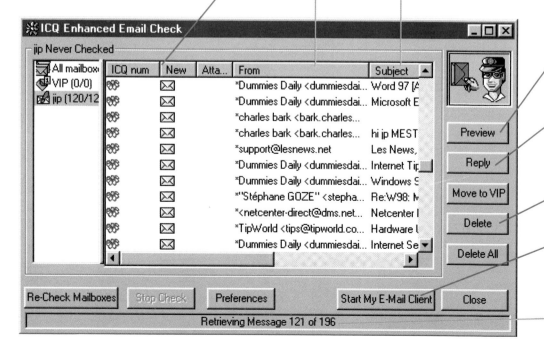

Communicate

ICQ offers several means of communicating. The main one is the same in all cases: select the user you wish to contact and click. Then select the desired command.

If the recipient is not online, the message remains in waiting either on the **ICQ** server or on your computer until the user is connected or available again.

Each time that a user tries to contact you in any way, his/her name or the **System** button will flash. Click on it twice to retrieve the communication addressed to you.

As anybody can get on the Internet, you risk being bothered or even harassed. **ICQ** enables you to ignore hostile users so that you are not disturbed.

TIP

Log a chat session with the File/Save Buffer command. ICQ will suggest that you create a text file to contain your chat.

HOW TO

A user need not be an ICQ subscriber to send you an express message. All s/he has to do is give the following address: UIN@pager.mirabilis.com For example: 12345667@pager.mirabilis.com

Note

To communicate with one of your contacts, click on that user's name: the menu offers the different communication options.

Warning

Not all ICQ versions have the same features. For example, the Macintosh version does not recognise telephone call requests. It is therefore possible that some features will be ineffective.

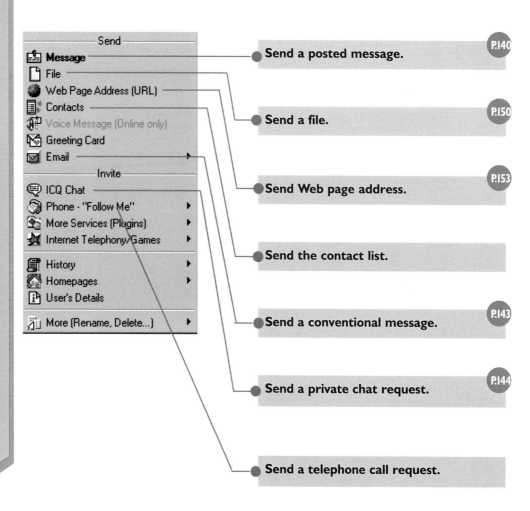

Send a posted message. **P.140**

Send a file. **P.150**

Send Web page address. **P.153**

Send the contact list.

Send a conventional message. **P.143**

Send a private chat request. **P.144**

Send a telephone call request.

Configure event reception

ICQ/Preferences & Security/Security (Events tab)

Notes

Click on the ICQ button and select Preferences & Security/Preferences. Now click on the Events tab

If the Auto Send Messages option is not active, messages for users not on line are kept on your computer until you are both connected (see page 140).

Select the type of event.

Options for the selected type of event.

Options are validated for all events.

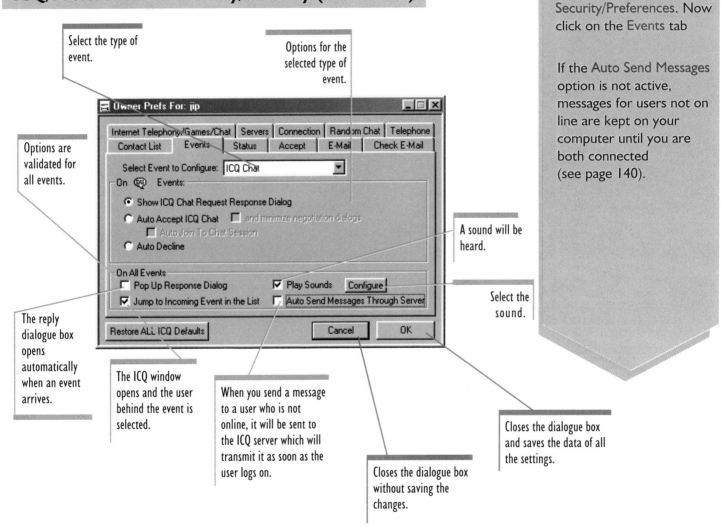

A sound will be heard.

Select the sound.

The reply dialogue box opens automatically when an event arrives.

The ICQ window opens and the user behind the event is selected.

When you send a message to a user who is not online, it will be sent to the ICQ server which will transmit it as soon as the user logs on.

Closes the dialogue box without saving the changes.

Closes the dialogue box and saves the data of all the settings.

Note

You are alerted that an event has arrived (message, chat request, file, etc.) by a sound, by the display of the message, by the opening of the ICQ window, by a small flashing message in the taskbar or in front of the user's name in the ICQ window. Make your choice: click on the ICQ button, select the Windows/Alerts command, and tick the types of notification in the Global Alerts field.

The arrival of each event can be set for each user individually. In the user menu, select the More/Alert/Accept Modes command.

Receive an event

ICQ/Windows-Alerts

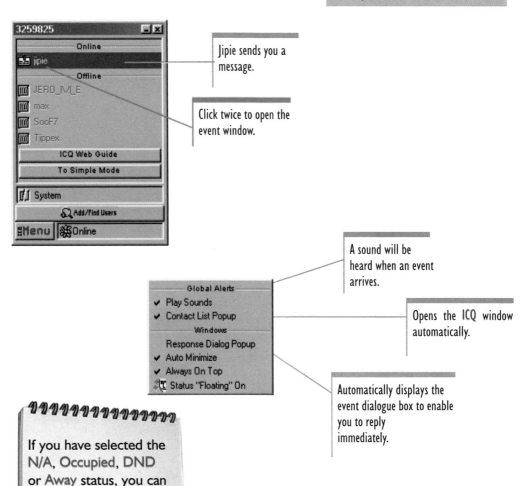

Jipie sends you a message.

Click twice to open the event window.

A sound will be heard when an event arrives.

Opens the ICQ window automatically.

Automatically displays the event dialogue box to enable you to reply immediately.

If you have selected the N/A, Occupied, DND or Away status, you can choose whether or not you wish to be informed about the arrival of messages. See page 126.

Send a posted message

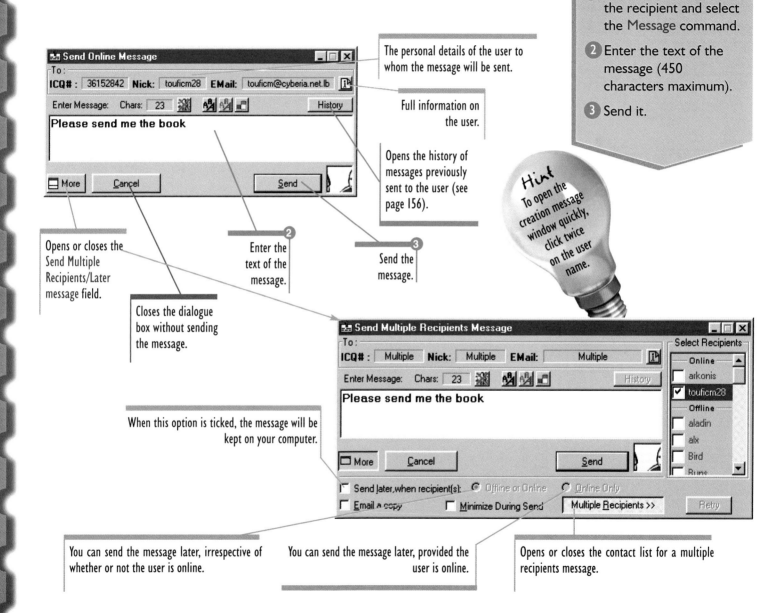

The personal details of the user to whom the message will be sent.

Full information on the user.

Opens the history of messages previously sent to the user (see page 156).

Opens or closes the Send Multiple Recipients/Later message field.

Closes the dialogue box without sending the message.

②
Enter the text of the message.

③
Send the message.

When this option is ticked, the message will be kept on your computer.

You can send the message later, irrespective of whether or not the user is online.

You can send the message later, provided the user is online.

Opens or closes the contact list for a multiple recipients message.

Checklist
1 Click on the name of the recipient and select the Message command.
2 Enter the text of the message (450 characters maximum).
3 Send it.

Hint
To open the creation message window quickly, click twice on the user name.

140

Notes

Click on the Font, Font Color and Background Color buttons.

The message will reach your contact as you see it in the window.

Personalise your posted messages

Message

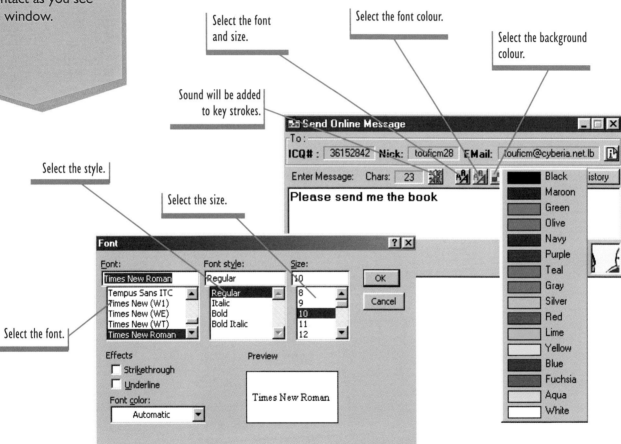

Select the font and size.

Select the font colour.

Select the background colour.

Sound will be added to key strokes.

Select the style.

Select the size.

Select the font.

Reply to a posted message

Personal details of message sender.

Text of the message.

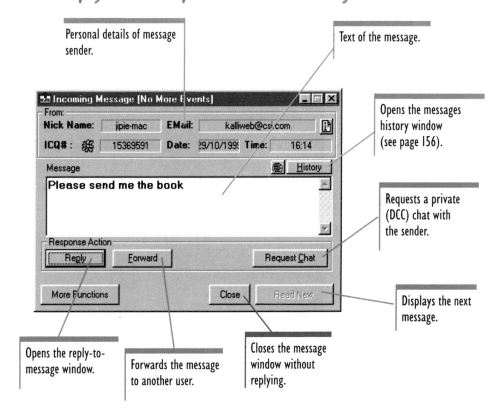

Opens the messages history window (see page 156).

Requests a private (DCC) chat with the sender.

Displays the next message.

Opens the reply-to-message window.

Forwards the message to another user.

Closes the message window without replying.

Notes

Click twice on the small message logo in the task-bar or in the ICQ window.

When several events are waiting, the title of the window indicates the number of events that you can still read by clicking on the Read Next button.

You do not have to be an ICQ user to send a posted message. You simply have to give the following as address: UIN pager.mirabilis.com. For example, the ICQ number of the author of this book is 3259825: you can send him a posted message at 3259825@pager.mirabilis.com. ICQ calls this type of message Email Express.

Indicate this express address in the signature of your e-mails so that you can be contacted quickly. You will receive the express messages as soon as you connect to an ICQ server.

Click on the name of the recipient and select the EMail/Send Email command.

Compose your message as normal in the create mail window of your e-mail software.

If the commands Send Email / Send Email + Notify By ICQ are shaded, the user did not enter his/her e-mail address in his/her details.

Send a standard E-mail

Email/Send Email

Click on this command.

Send a message to the user's mailbox.

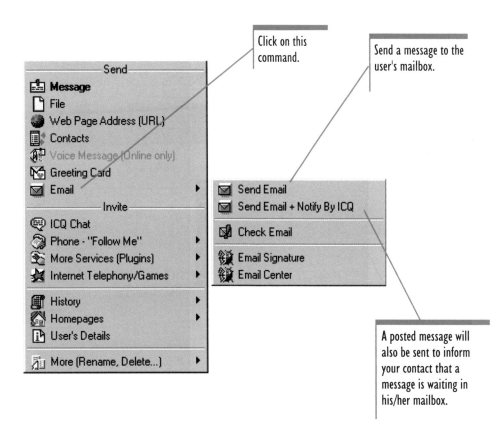

A posted message will also be sent to inform your contact that a message is waiting in his/her mailbox.

Request a private chat

ICQ Chat

Checklist

1 Click on the user with whom you wish to chat and select the ICQ Chat command.

2 Enter a message to accompany your request.

3 Send the request.

When your contact agrees to chat, the chat window will open (see page 149).

Enter the chat subject.

Details of the user to whom you send the chat request.

Opens a dialogue box containing all the user's information.

If the user is not online, this option enables you to send the request which will be forwarded as soon as they connect.

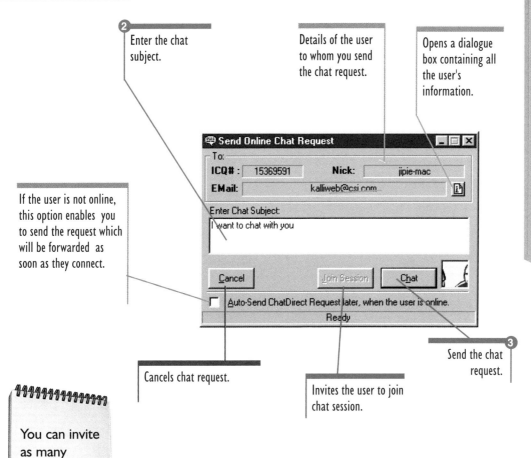

Cancels chat request.

Invites the user to join chat session.

Send the chat request.

Your contact declines the chat request.

You can invite as many persons as you wish to a chat session.

To invite a user to a chat session, drag his or her name from the contacts list into the chat window.

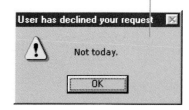

Click twice on the small bubble in the taskbar or in front of the name of the user who has sent you the message.

When you agree to chat, the chat window opens.

Details of user requesting the chat.

Window containing the user's full details.

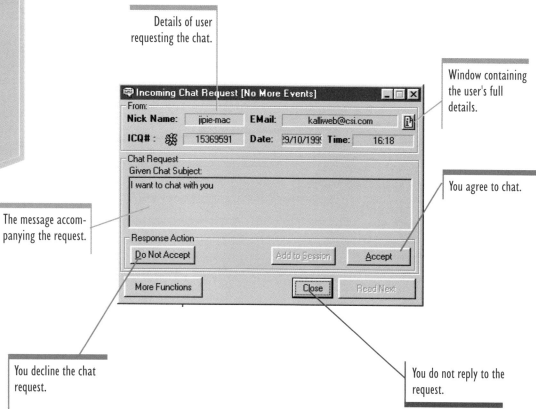

The message accompanying the request.

You agree to chat.

You decline the chat request.

You do not reply to the request.

You are free for a chat

Free For Chat

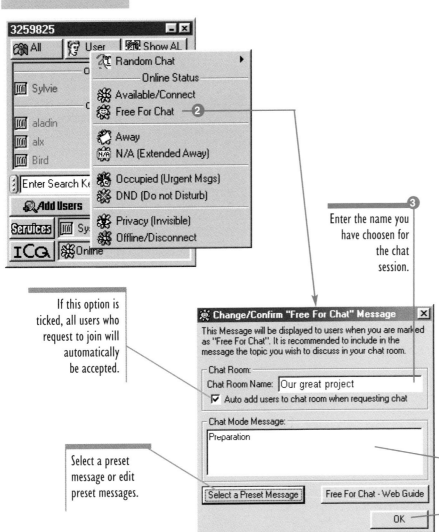

If this option is ticked, all users who request to join will automatically be accepted.

Enter the name you have choosen for the chat session.

Select a preset message or edit preset messages.

Enter the chat subject.

Confirm your 'Free for Chat' status.

Checklist

1. Click the Status button and select the Free For Chat command.

2. In a contact list, the names of those free for chat is preceded by the small chat icon.

3. Enter the name you have chosen for the chat session.

4. Enter a topic here you wish to discuss. Your contacts can read the chat subject and must then make a chat request: they can simply click on your name and deselect the Read Chat Room Message command.

5. Finally, click OK to confirm your 'Free for Chat' status.

Checklist

1. To define your availability settings, click on the Status button in the ICQ window and select Random chat/My Random Chat Settings.

2. In the dialogue box, tick I want to be available ...

3. Enter your nickname and add a few comments to be read by random chat users: your language, sex and so on.

4. Click on Save.

5. To activate (or deactivate) your available-for-random-chat status, click on the Status button in the ICQ window and select Random chat/Available for Random Chat.

Random Chat/Available For Random Chat

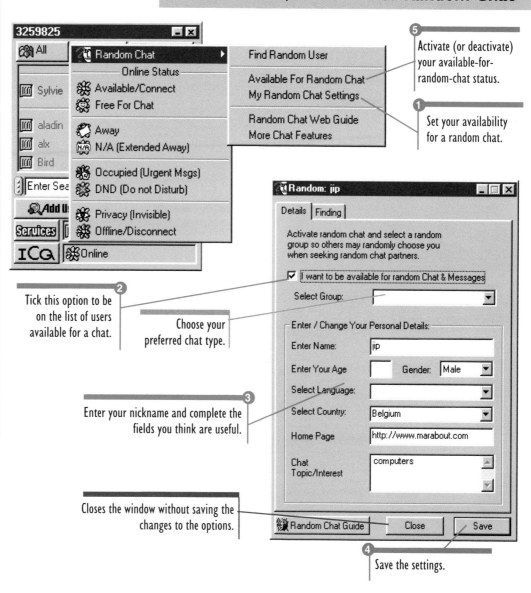

Activate (or deactivate) your available-for-random-chat status.

Set your availability for a random chat.

Tick this option to be on the list of users available for a chat.

Choose your preferred chat type.

Enter your nickname and complete the fields you think are useful.

Closes the window without saving the changes to the options.

Save the settings.

Find a random chat

Random Chat/Find Random User

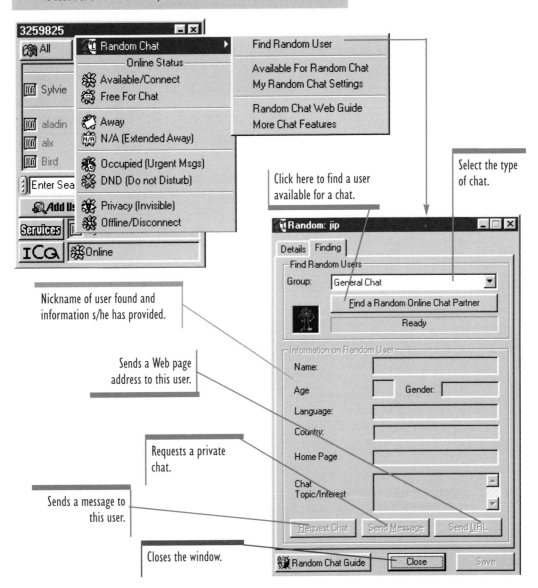

Nickname of user found and information s/he has provided.

Sends a Web page address to this user.

Requests a private chat.

Sends a message to this user.

Closes the window.

Click here to find a user available for a chat.

Select the type of chat.

Notes

Click on the Status button in the ICQ window and select Find Random User.

Click on Find a Random Online Chat Partner.

If the user found is not suitable, click once again on Find a Random Online Chat Partner.

If you do not wish to receive any more chat requests or messages from a particular user who is annoying you, enter him/her in the list of users to ignore (see page 157).

Notes

The chat window functions in two modes: the IRC mode or the split mode. Select the mode from the Layout menu.

In IRC mode, each message you enter is sent when you press Enter.

In split mode, each character is sent as you type it.

Each user chooses his/her mode independently of the other users.

A chat session in split mode

You are away from the keyboard. The chat window is minimised and all the other users receive the message 'User is away.'

The next characters will be in boldface, italics or underlined.

Enlarges/reduces the font size.

Select font.

Changes the background colour of your pane.

Changes the colour of the next characters you enter.

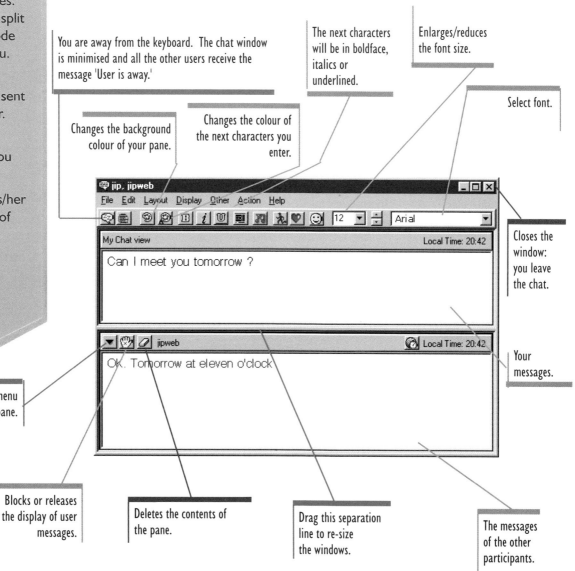

Closes the window: you leave the chat.

Your messages.

Opens a command menu for the user in this pane.

Blocks or releases the display of user messages.

Deletes the contents of the pane.

Drag this separation line to re-size the windows.

The messages of the other participants.

Send a file

File

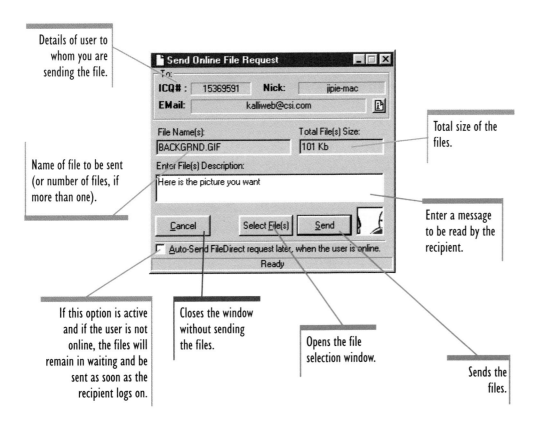

Details of user to whom you are sending the file.

Name of file to be sent (or number of files, if more than one).

Total size of the files.

Enter a message to be read by the recipient.

If this option is active and if the user is not online, the files will remain in waiting and be sent as soon as the recipient logs on.

Closes the window without sending the files.

Opens the file selection window.

Sends the files.

Notes

Click on the name of the user to whom you wish to send a file and select the File command.

Select the file to send.

Click on the Open button.

Type the message to the recipient.

Click on the Send button.

To send a file or a folder, drag its icon onto the name of the user.
To send a file, click on the icon with the right mouse button, select ICQ-Send to user first and then the name of the recipient.

Notes

The user to whom you sent the files may accept or decline them.

As soon as s/he accepts the file, the transmission window opens.

Your contact receives your files

File transfer progress.

Name of file being sent.

Location of file in your computer.

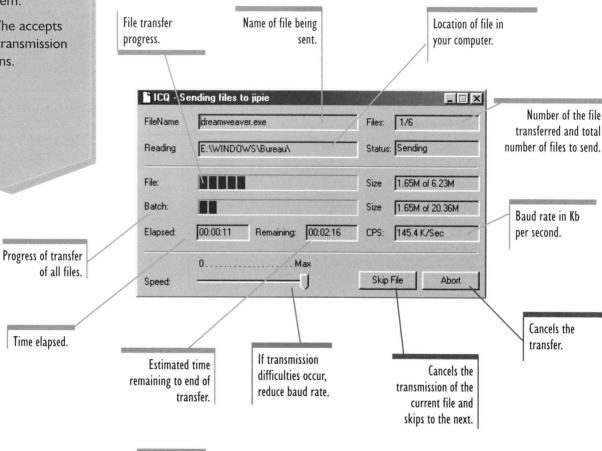

Number of the file transferred and total number of files to send.

Baud rate in Kb per second.

Progress of transfer of all files.

Time elapsed.

Estimated time remaining to end of transfer.

If transmission difficulties occur, reduce baud rate.

Cancels the transmission of the current file and skips to the next.

Cancels the transfer.

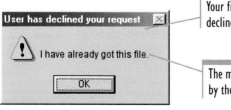

Your files are declined.

The message sent by the user.

Receive a file

Notes

Notes

Click twice on the small file icon in the taskbar or in front of the name of the contact sending you the file.

When you agree to receive the files, the transfer window opens: it is identical to the window that opens when you send files.

The files are saved by default in a folder bearing the name of the sender and located at \ICQ\Received file.

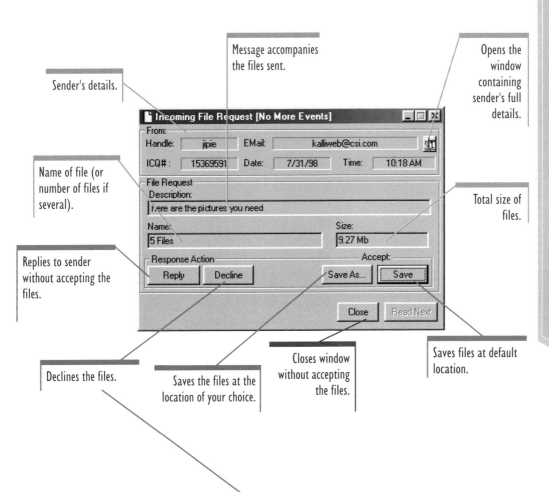

Message accompanies the files sent.

Opens the window containing sender's full details.

Sender's details.

Name of file (or number of files if several).

Total size of files.

Replies to sender without accepting the files.

Declines the files.

Saves the files at the location of your choice.

Closes window without accepting the files.

Saves files at default location.

Incoming File Request [No More Events]

From:
Handle: jipie   EMail: kalliweb@csi.com
ICQ#: 15369591   Date: 7/31/98   Time: 10:18 AM

File Request
Description:
Here are the pictures you need

Name: Size:
5 Files   9.27 Mb

Response Action   Accept:
Reply   Decline   Save As...   Save

Close   Read Next

Decline - without given a reason.
Decline - "Sorry but I am busy right now. Can't respond to your request."
Decline - "Sorry but I am busy right now. I will send you a request when I'm done"
Away - reply with an away message
Enter a decline reason

Checklist

1. Click on the name of the user to whom you wish to send a file, and select the command **Web Page Address (URL)**.

2. Enter the address.

3. Enter an accompanying. message.

4. Send.

Send a Web page address (URL)

Web Page Address (URL)

Recipient's details.

Opens the window containing recipient's full details.

Enter or select the address.

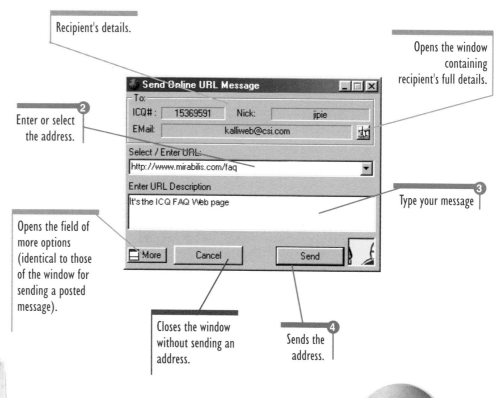

Send Online URL Message

To:
ICQ# : 15369591   Nick: jipie
EMail: kalliweb@csi.com

Select / Enter URL:
http://www.mirabilis.com/faq

Enter URL Description
It's the ICQ FAQ Web page

More   Cancel   Send

Type your message

Opens the field of more options (identical to those of the window for sending a posted message).

Closes the window without sending an address.

Sends the address.

Send only URLs and make sure they are complete. For example: do not send www.marabout.com but rather http://www.marabout.com

To send a URL to one of your contacts, drag its link from the Internet browser window to the name of the contact.

153

Receive a Web page address

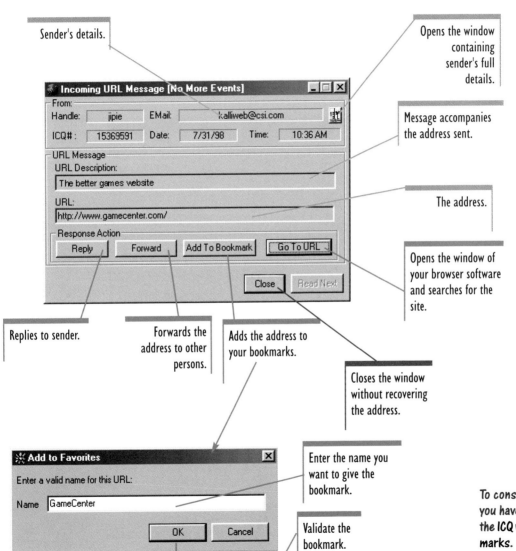

Sender's details.

Opens the window containing sender's full details.

Message accompanies the address sent.

The address.

Opens the window of your browser software and searches for the site.

Replies to sender.

Forwards the address to other persons.

Adds the address to your bookmarks.

Closes the window without recovering the address.

Enter the name you want to give the bookmark.

Validate the bookmark.

Notes

Click twice on the earth icon in the taskbar or in front of the name of the contact sending you the address.

The addresses you wish to add to your bookmarks are entered in the From ICQ folder of the Internet Explorer Favorites.

To consult the list of bookmarks you have received, click on **System** in the **ICQ** window and select **Incoming Bookmarks.**

System/History and Outbox (Outbox tab)

When you send a message, a file or a Web page address by selecting the Compose Now-Autosend later option (available by clicking on More in the message creation window), the message remains in your computer's Outbox.

To see the messages in the Outbox, click on the System button and select the History and Outbox command; then click on the Outbox tab.

Click twice on an event to see its full contents.

List of events in the Outbox.

Sends messages immediately. If the recipient is online, all the messages are sent to him/her. If s/he is not online, only the messages with Online or Offline status are sent.

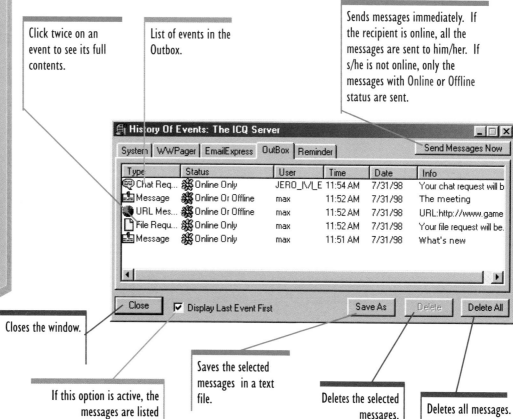

Closes the window.

If this option is active, the messages are listed chronologically in decreasing order by the date and time they were created.

Saves the selected messages in a text file.

Deletes the selected messages.

Deletes all messages.

Hint
Click twice on the System menu in the ICQ window.

Messages history

History/View Messages History

Click to list by column contents.

Events from the user.

Events you sent to the user.

Message exchanges.

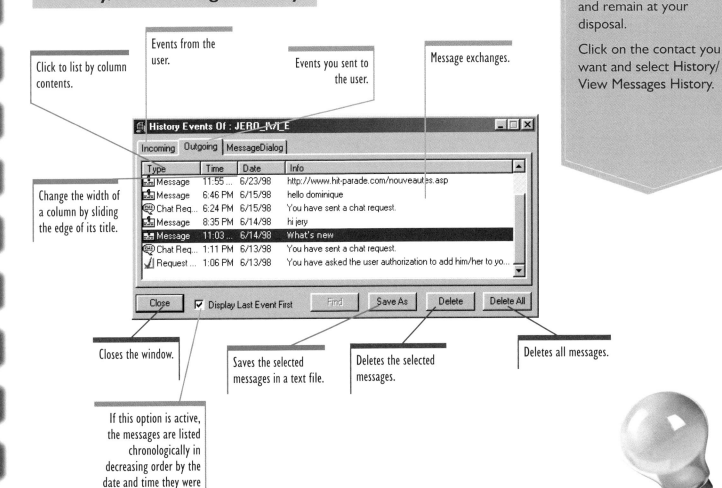

Change the width of a column by sliding the edge of its title.

History Events Of : JERO_W_E

| Incoming | Outgoing | MessageDialog |

Type	Time	Date	Info
Message	11:55 ...	6/23/98	http://www.hit-parade.com/nouveautes.asp
Message	6:46 PM	6/15/98	hello dominique
Chat Req...	6:24 PM	6/15/98	You have sent a chat request.
Message	8:35 PM	6/14/98	hi jery
Message	11:03 ...	6/14/98	What's new
Chat Req...	1:11 PM	6/13/98	You have sent a chat request.
Request ...	1:06 PM	6/13/98	You have asked the user authorization to add him/her to yo...

Close   ☑ Display Last Event First   Find   Save As   Delete   Delete All

Closes the window.

Saves the selected messages in a text file.

Deletes the selected messages.

Deletes all messages.

If this option is active, the messages are listed chronologically in decreasing order by the date and time they were created.

To obtain the messages history in relation to the system, click on the System button and select History and Outbox. The System tab contains the events relative to the ICQ and the servers.

ICQ/Security & Privacy (Ignore List)

Notes

Click on the ICQ button and select Preferences & Security/Security & Privacy. Then click on the Ignore List tab.

A user in the Ignore list is automatically extracted from your contact list. S/he no longer exists for you.

A removed user is not automatically reinserted in the contact list. You have to enter him/her again.

Only messages from users in your contact list will be accepted. The others will be ignored.

Declines messages sent to several users simultaneously (anti-spam option).

Declines all direct communication with users with a previous ICQ version (the security settings are less efficient in preceding versions).

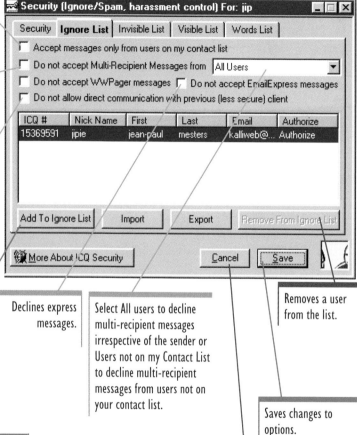

Declines express messages.

Add a user to the list.

Search for him/her.

Enter the e-mail address, the name or the ICQ number of the user.

Click twice on his/her name to insert it into the list.

Select All users to decline multi-recipient messages irrespective of the sender or Users not on my Contact List to decline multi-recipient messages from users not on your contact list.

Removes a user from the list.

Saves changes to options.

Cancels all changes to options. Warning: additions to or deletions from the list are never cancelled.

Configure ICQ

The **ICQ** network is maintained by several inter-connected servers. Each user can connect to any server. **ICQ** proposes some default servers, but you can complete the list with a series of other servers.

Furthermore, if the same computer is used by several persons, it is preferable for each of them to have his or her own **ICQ** number. **ICQ** has the ability to save and keep in storage the settings, files, and messages of 8 users at most. Click on the **ICQ** button and select the **Add/Change Current User** command.

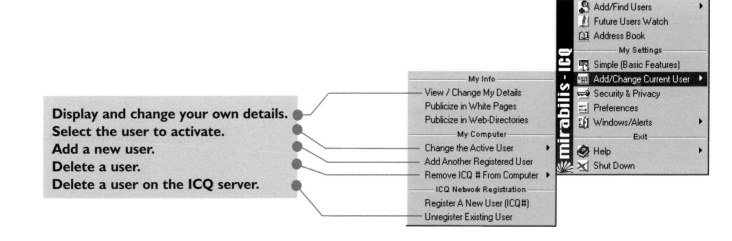

Display and change your own details.
Select the user to activate.
Add a new user.
Delete a user.
Delete a user on the ICQ server.

Notes

Click on the ICQ button and select Preferences & Security/Preferences. Click on the Servers tab.

When attempting to connect, ICQ tries the servers in the order they are displayed in this list.

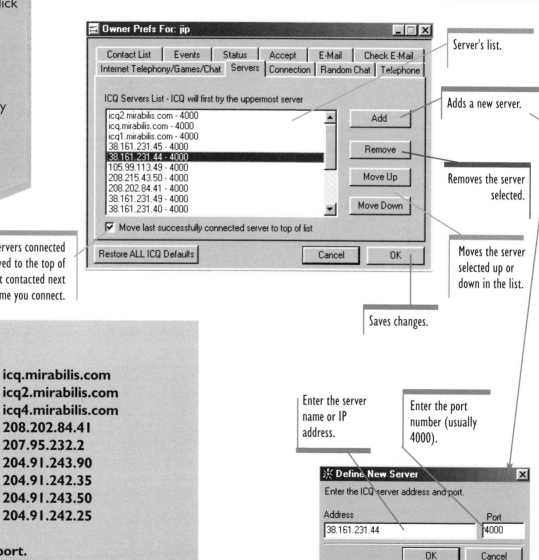

Server's list.

Adds a new server.

Removes the server selected.

Moves the server selected up or down in the list.

Saves changes.

If this option is active, the servers connected successfully are automatically moved to the top of the list. They will be the first contacted next time you connect.

Enter the server name or IP address.

Enter the port number (usually 4000).

The ICQ servers

icqalpha.mirabilis.com	icq.mirabilis.com
icq1.mirabilis.com	icq2.mirabilis.com
icq3.mirabilis.com	icq4.mirabilis.com
icq5.mirabilis.com	208.202.84.41
208.215.43.50	207.95.232.2
204.91.243.41	204.91.243.90
204.91.243.112	204.91.242.35
204.91.243.77	204.91.243.50
204.91.242.80	204.91.242.25

All severs use the 4000 port.

Chapter 4

ICQ for Macintosh

Introducing ICQ for Macintosh

The ICQ version for Macintosh is very similar to the version which runs under Windows, but offers fewer options and commands. In this chapter we deal only with the differences in relation to the Windows version. For the similar properties, please refer to the preceding chapter.

Publisher: Mirabilis
Publisher's website: http://www.mirabilis.com
ICQ site: http://www.icq.com
Shareware
System requirements: PowerMac or Mac 68 K (there is a version for each Macintosh model)
Download from:

http://www.icq.com/download/step-by-step-mac.html (for PowerMac) - 1,6 Mb

http://www.icq.com/download/step-by-step-mac68.html (for Mac 68 K) - 1,5 Mb

TIP

What can you do with ICQ for Macintosh?

Be notified when another ICQ subscriber logs on to the Internet.

Notify other users of your presence on the Internet.

Send to and receive quick messages from ICQ users.

Send and receive files.

Send and receive Web page addresses.

Chat.

The registration procedure is identical to that of the Windows version (see page 107).

The ICQ window

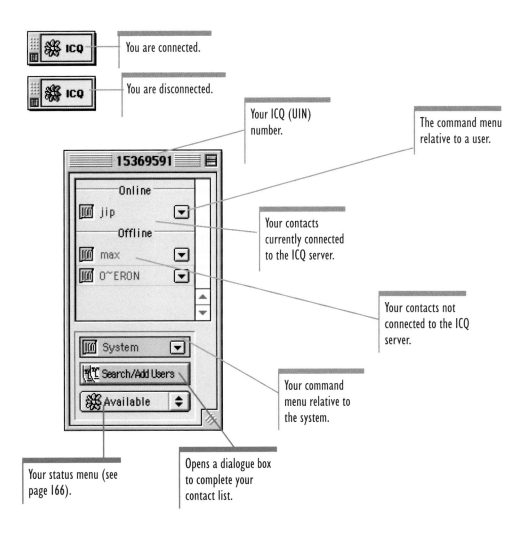

You are connected.

You are disconnected.

Your ICQ (UIN) number.

The command menu relative to a user.

15369591

Online

jip

Offline

max

O~ERON

System

Search/Add Users

Available

Your contacts currently connected to the ICQ server.

Your contacts not connected to the ICQ server.

Your command menu relative to the system.

Your status menu (see page 166).

Opens a dialogue box to complete your contact list.

Notes

The small floating window indicates the connection status.

It always remains in the foreground. Click on it twice to bring the ICQ window to the foreground again.

To close (or redisplay) the small floating window, select the Windows/ICQ Floater command.

Close the ICQ session with the File/Quit command.

To launch ICQ automatically when you start your computer, place the ICQ alias in the Startup folder (located in the System folder).

Your presence online

When you are connected to one of the **ICQ** servers, you are, in principle, visible and can be contacted by subscribers who have your name in their contact list. In reality, you are free to choose a status: 'Do not disturb', 'Away' or 'Privacy' for all the users or for certain users only.

Furthermore, when another subscriber wants to add you to his/her contact list, you may request that it is not done automatically: your authorisation will then be required.

If you assume the Away or Occupied status, a message will be sent to the users who try to contact you. You will be notified only about the arrival of urgent messages. The other messages will remain in waiting until you are available again.

Your **ICQ** subscription does not preclude you from taking other security measures (for example : it does not hide your IP address). While remaining available to other users, you can take certain precautions that will shelter you from unwelcome intruders.

HOW TO

Use the Privacy mode to remain connected to the ICQ network while appearing to be absent for the other users.

TIP

The data provided by your contacts are not necessarily reliable.

Do not be too quick to trust strangers.

- Available
- Away
- Occupied
- Privacy (Invisible)
- Offline

Your presence online

Select your status.

The Offline status is automatically activated when you disconnect from the Internet. The status you had when you disconnected will be automatically reactivated next time you connect.

The ICQ symbol in the small floating window reflects your status.

Online	You are online and everybody can contact you.
Away	You are away from your keyboard for a short period. You are therefore not available, but are still online. Users who try to contact you will receive the message you have prepared. The messages they sent to you will be waiting until you return.
Occupied	You are occupied and do not wish to be disturbed unnecessarily. The message you have prepared will be sent to the users who try to contact you. You will be notified only if urgent messages come in. The other messages will remain waiting until you are available again.
Privacy	The other users see your name in their **Offline** list, although you are still online.
Offline	You have disconnected from the **ICQ** server.

Complete your contact list by clicking on the Search/Add Users button.

166

Notes

Select the File/Preferences command and click on the Status tab.

You can prepare a message for the Away status and another message for the Occupied status. They will be sent to users who wish to contact you while one of these statuses is active.

Closes the dialogue box.

Select the mode for which you wish to create a message.

Enter the message that will be displayed to the users who try to contact you while you are in Occupied or Away mode.

A beep will sound when you receive a message while in Occupied mode.

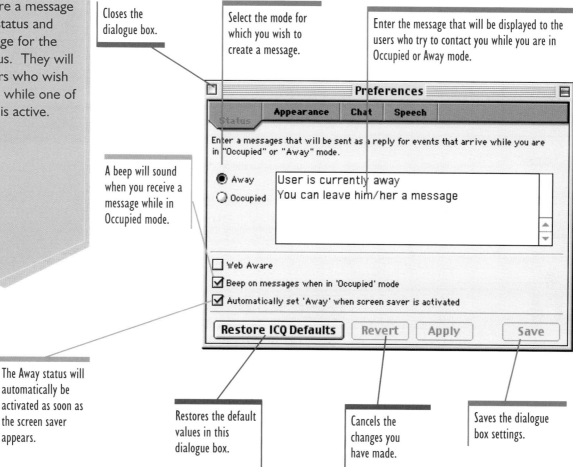

Preferences

| Status | Appearance | Chat | Speech |

Enter a messages that will be sent as a reply for events that arrive while you are in "Occupied" or "Away" mode.

◉ Away
○ Occupied

User is currently away
You can leave him/her a message

☐ Web Aware
☑ Beep on messages when in 'Occupied' mode
☑ Automatically set 'Away' when screen saver is activated

Restore ICQ Defaults　　Revert　　Apply　　Save

The Away status will automatically be activated as soon as the screen saver appears.

Restores the default values in this dialogue box.

Cancels the changes you have made.

Saves the dialogue box settings.

Your details

File/View-Change my details

Note
In the File menu, select Change my details.

Change your details in the Main, Address, More and About tabs of this dialogue box.

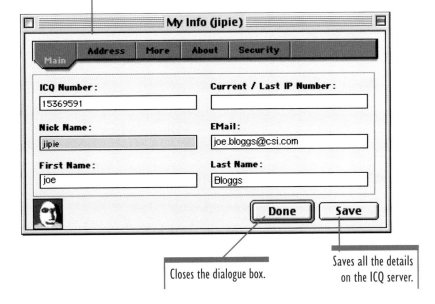

My Info (jipie)

| Main | Address | More | About | Security |

ICQ Number:
15369591

Current / Last IP Number:

Nick Name:
jipie

EMail:
joe.bloggs@csi.com

First Name:
joe

Last Name:
Bloggs

Done   Save

Closes the dialogue box.

Saves all the details on the ICQ server.

Your details can be read by any ICQ subscriber, so be careful and only enter information that is really necessary.

168

Note

In the File menu, select Change my details and then click on the Security tab.

File/Change my details (Security tab)

Select an option:
the first (anyone can enter you in his/her contact list without asking for your authorisation) or the second (to include you in his/her contact list, a subscriber must ask for your authorisation first).

Change your password if you wish.

Enter your password once again to confirm it.

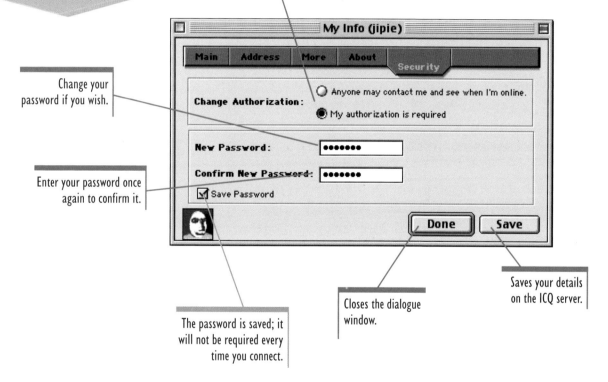

The password is saved; it will not be required every time you connect.

Closes the dialogue window.

Saves your details on the ICQ server.

169

Communicate

ICQ offers several means of communicating: posted messages transmitted immediately from one user to another; conventional messages sent to the recipient's mailbox; chat; and transmission of files, web page addresses or user details.

The principle is the same in all cases: open the menu of the user you wish to contact and click. Then select the commands that interest you.

If the recipient is not online, or if s/he is not available, the message remains waiting either on the **ICQ** server or on your computer until the user is connected or available again.

Each time that a user tries to contact you in any way, his/her name or the System button will flash. Click on it twice to read the communication addressed to you.

HOW TO

Anyone can send you an express message. All s/he has to do is give the following address: UIN@pager.mirabilis.com
For example:
1234567@pager.mirabilis.com

TIP

In the chat window, paste text you want to copy in another application.

Use the clipboard commands from the Edit menu.

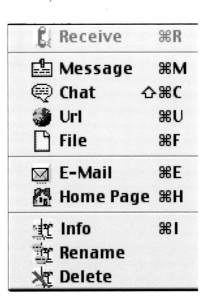

🔔 Receive	⌘R
📇 Message	⌘M
💬 Chat	⇧⌘C
🌐 Url	⌘U
📄 File	⌘F
✉ E-Mail	⌘E
🖼 Home Page	⌘H
Info	⌘I
Rename	
Delete	

Checklist

1. Open the recipient menu in your contact list.

2. Select Message.

3. Enter the text of the message.

4. Click the Send button to send it.

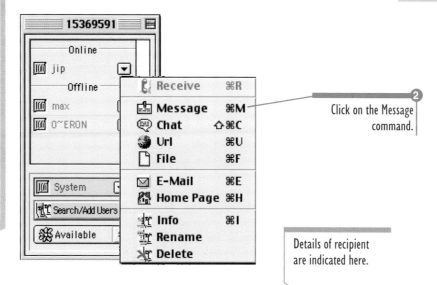

Click on the Message command.

Details of recipient are indicated here.

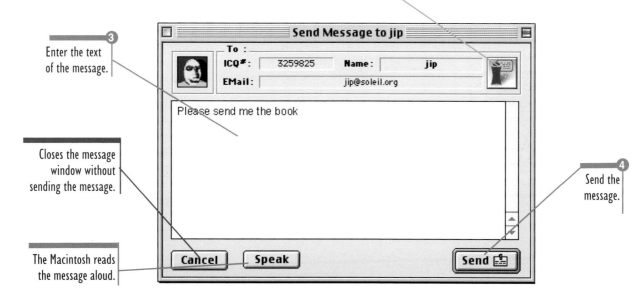

Enter the text of the message.

Closes the message window without sending the message.

The Macintosh reads the message aloud.

Send the message.

171

Receive a posted message

Note

To open the message, click on the small message image flashing in the ICQ window.

Details of sender are indicated here.

Opens the window containing the full details of the sender.

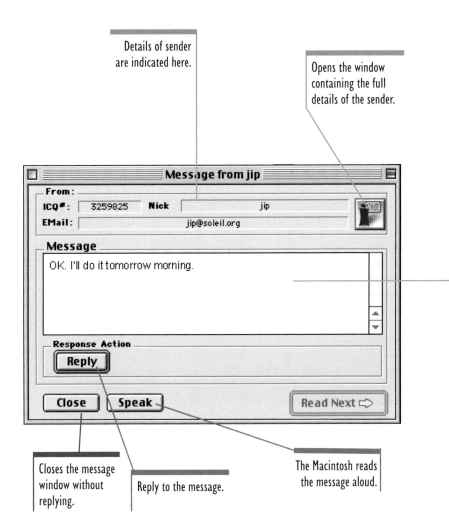

Text of the message.

Closes the message window without replying.

Reply to the message.

The Macintosh reads the message aloud.

Checklist

1. Open the recipient's menu in your contact list.

2. Select the Chat command.

3. Enter the message accompanying your request.

4. Click on the Chat button.

   If your contact accepts, the Chat window will open.

Send a chat request

Chat

Send a chat request to a user whose details are indicated here.

Opens the window containing the full details of the user.

Enter message accompanying your request.

Closes the window without sending the chat request.

Send the request.

Your contact has refused.

Receive a chat request

Note

To open the chat request, click twice on the small flashing ball in the ICQ window.

Details of user requesting the chat.

Opens the window containing the full details of the user.

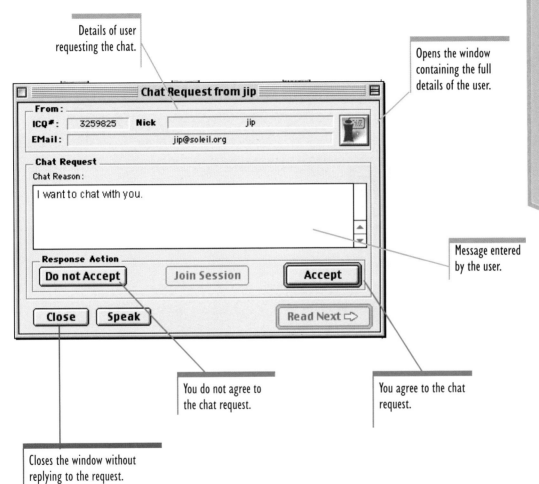

Message entered by the user.

You do not agree to the chat request.

You agree to the chat request.

Closes the window without replying to the request.

Notes

You can use the clipboard as in any application. The commands are in the Edit menu: Cut, Copy and Paste.

First select the text to copy and paste.

Select your message text colour.

Select the background colour of your message window.

Enter the text you want to send to the other participants in your window.

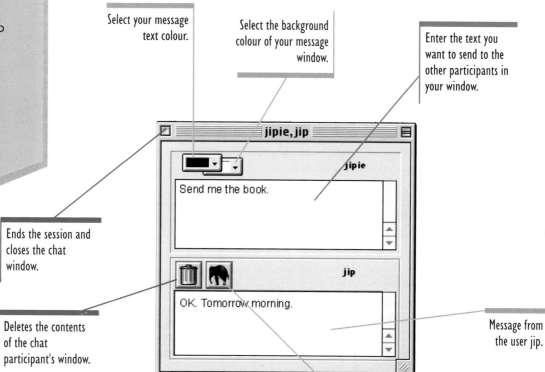

Ends the session and closes the chat window.

Deletes the contents of the chat participant's window.

Message from the user jip.

Sends a sound signal to the participant.

Select the **Chat/Beep User** command to send a sound signal to the participants.

Send a Web page address

URL

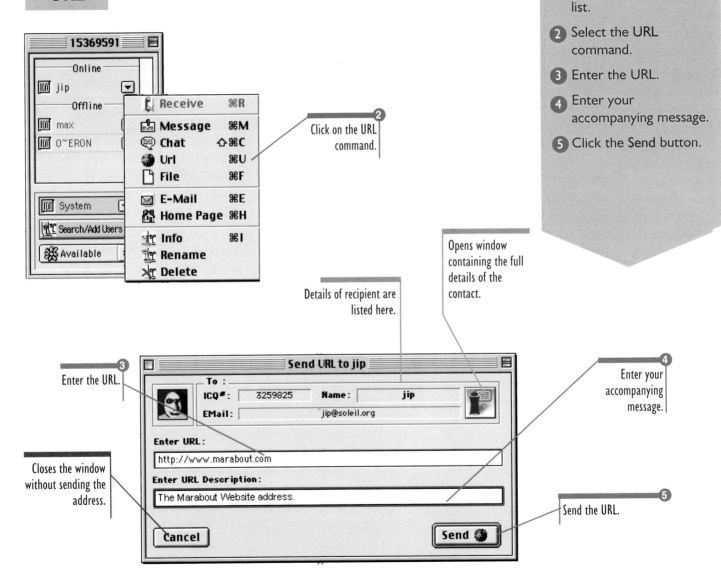

Click on the URL command.

Details of recipient are listed here.

Opens window containing the full details of the contact.

Enter the URL.

Closes the window without sending the address.

Enter your accompanying message.

Send the URL.

Checklist

1 Open the recipient's menu in your contact list.

2 Select the URL command.

3 Enter the URL.

4 Enter your accompanying message.

5 Click the Send button.

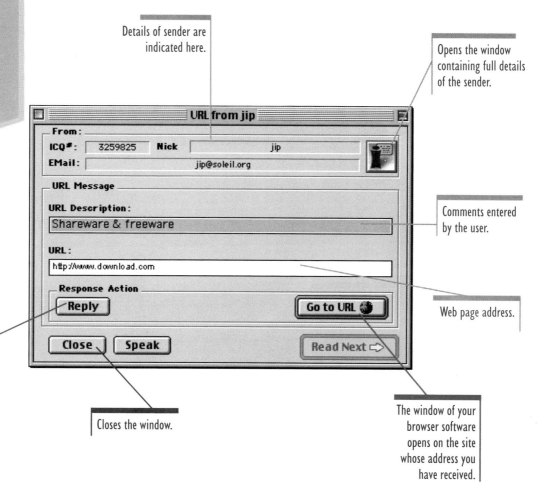
Notes

To receive a URL, click twice on the earth image flashing in the ICQ window.

Click on the **Go To URL** button to visit the proposed site.

Details of sender are indicated here.

Opens the window containing full details of the sender.

Comments entered by the user.

Web page address.

Send a posted message to sender.

Closes the window.

The window of your browser software opens on the site whose address you have received.

URL from jip

From:
ICQ#: 3259825   Nick   jip
EMail: jip@soleil.org

URL Message

URL Description:
Shareware & freeware

URL:
http://www.download.com

Response Action

[Reply]   [Go to URL]

[Close] [Speak]   [Read Next ➪]

Send files

File

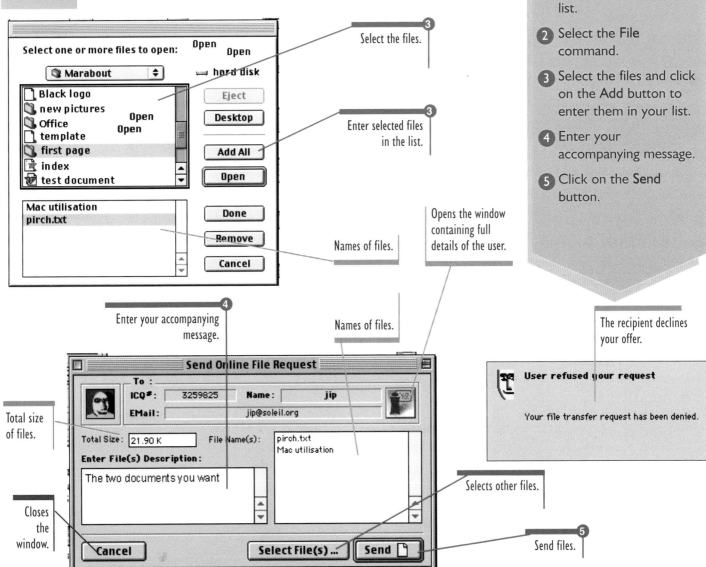

Select the files.

Enter selected files in the list.

Names of files.

Opens the window containing full details of the user.

Enter your accompanying message.

Names of files.

Total size of files.

Closes the window.

Selects other files.

Send files.

Checklist

1. Open the recipient's menu in your contact list.

2. Select the **File** command.

3. Select the files and click on the Add button to enter them in your list.

4. Enter your accompanying message.

5. Click on the **Send** button.

The recipient declines your offer.

User refused your request

Your file transfer request has been denied.

Note

As soon as the recipient accepts the files, the **Outgoing File Transfer** window opens and displays the transfer status.

Name of the file being transferred.

Outgoing file number and total number of files to send.

File transfer progress.

Outgoing File Transfer

File Name: 315   Files: 4/8

Reading: 315   Status: Sending

File: ▭▭▭   Size: 28 K of 110.47 K

Progress of transfer of all files.

Batch: ▭▭▭   Size: 80.85 K of 233.15 K

Elapsed: 00:00:04   Remaining: 00:00:07   CPS: 20.7 K/Sec

Baud rate in Kb per second.

Speed: ▭▭▭   Skip File   Abort

Time elapsed.

If transmission difficulties occur, reduce baud rate.

Estimated time remaining to end of transfer.

Cancels the transfer of the current file and skips to the next.

Aborts the transfer procedure.

179

Receive files

Notes

To receive files, click twice on the small file flashing in the **ICQ** window.

When you agree to receive the files the transfer window opens; it is identical to the window that opens when you send files.

Details of sender.

Opens the window containing full details of the sender.

Message accompanying the files.

Name of file (or number of files if several).

Total size of files.

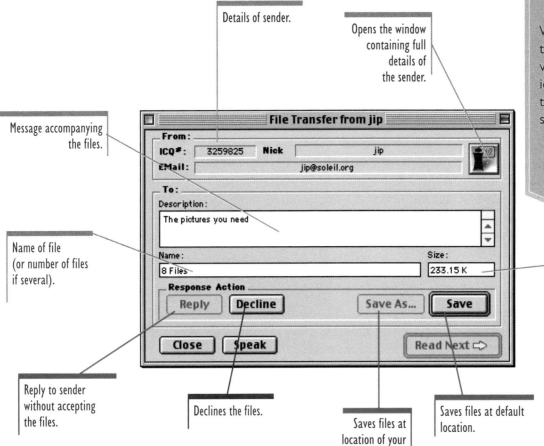

Reply to sender without accepting the files.

Declines the files.

Saves files at location of your choice.

Saves files at default location.

Appendix

Jargon and glossary

Jargon

All users of IRC channels, Newsgroups and other means of communication use and abuse a jargon composed of abbreviations, acronyms and homonyms. These often save time but above all, using them proves you are no longer a "newbie". Here are a few examples. Learn to decipher and to use them.

2l8	Too late
4me	For me
afk	Away from keyboard
aka	Also known as
asap	As soon as possible
bbl	Be back later
bot	Robot
brb	Be right back
chan	Channel
g	Sarcastic smile
IC	I see
imho	In my humble opinion
irl	In real life (as opposed to virtual life)
lol	Laughing out loud
mompl	Moment please
msg me	Send me a private message
nope	No
op	Operator
rl	Real life

rotfl	Rolling on the floor laughing
rsn	Real soon now
rtfm	Read the f**#!# manual
vl	Virtual life
w8	Wait

Some smileys

:-)	I am smiling, I am happy, I find it funny.	;-)	I am joking.
'-)	I am winking.	:->	I am being sarcastic.
:-/	I am sceptical.	:-S	I am talking nonsense.
:-I	I am indifferent.	:-(	I am sad; dissatisfied.
%-)	I am half asleep.	:#)	I am drunk.
:'-(	I am crying.	:'-)	I am dying of laughter.
:*	Kiss.	:*)	Kiss on the cheek.
:-*	I'll give you a kiss.	:-o	I am screaming.
:-<	I am very sad.	:-X	Big kiss.
:-C	I am dissatisfied.	:-D	I am making fun of you.
@--,--'---	Symbolises a rose. You are sending flowers.		

JARGON

Glossary

ban	Expulsion of a user from a channel for a specified period. Only operators can ban.
bankick	Ban followed by a kick (IRC).
banlist	List of users banned from the channel (IRC).
baud	Unit measuring the number of signaling elements per second on a telephone line.
bit	Abbreviation for binary digit. The smallest unit of information. A single bit can only hold one of two values : 0 or 1.
bot	See *robot*.
chan	See *channel*.
channel	Place of discussion offered by an IRC server. Synonymous with room.
chanop	Operator of an IRC channel.
client	Software or machine connected to a server.
clone	The double of a user in an IRC network. S/he is connected to the same network through several servers. This makes it possible to distribute or multiply the effect of floods and to remain present in case of a split.
codec	Compressor-decompressor of audio and video data.
CService	Channel registration service in an Undernet.
CTCP	Client To Client Protocol. CTCP commands are used to obtain information on a user or a server (IRC).
DalNet	One of the four European IRC networks.
DCC	Direct Client Connection. The DCC procedures used for private (DCC) chats and file transfer between users and outside the IRC network. The two users are connected without an intermediary.
Deop	Remove the status of channel operator from a user (IRC).
DND	Do Not Disturb (ICQ).
Domain	The name of your access provider, e.g. uk.net
EFNet	One of the four European IRC networks.

express email	An express message sent by a non-subscriber using the address UIN@pager.mirabilis.com. For example: 3259825@pager.mirabilis.com (ICQ).
flood	Dispatch of a large number of lines of texts or commands (more than 4) in a very short period of time. A flood generally earns a kick (IRC).
host	A computer system containing data accessed by a user from a remote location.
ICQ	Online presence program published by Mirabilis.
ICQ#	See *Universal Internet Number*.
Internet Relay Chat	Network for real-time chat.
Internet Relay Chat Daemon	IRC server.
Intranet	Local area network based on the TCP/IP protocol used on the Internet. An intranet is a private Internet.
IP Address	Address of a computer or a domain in numeric form. All users connected to the Internet receive an IP address which may be different for each connection. For example: 130.104.12.78
IRC	See *Internet Relay Chat*.
IRCD	See *Internet Relay Chat Daemon*.
IRCNet	One of the four European IRC networks.
IRCop	IRC server operator. The nickname of IRCops is preceded by an asterisk *.
kick	Expulsion of a user from an IRC channel. Light reprimand. The user can return to the channel immediately.
kill	Disconnection of a user from the IRC network.
lag	Delay between sending and receiving in an IRC network. This lag is caused by message transfer delays between servers. To cancel the lag with another user, you must connect to the same server as that user. There is no lag on the same server. To find out the server of a user, use the /whois command.
LAN	Local Area Network. Local network operating at great speed over short distances.
log	Recording of a discussion.
mainstream	Public window of a channel. This is the first window that opens when you enter a channel.

mode	Characteristic of a channel or a user. Modes can be changed only by the operators and are attributed with the /mode command (IRC).
N/A	Not Available. Presence status indicating that the user is temporarily not available (ICQ).
newbie	A beginner. A term often used with a pejorative connotation.
nick	Nickname assumed by a user to join a communication network (IRC for instance).
nickname	See *nick*.
offline	Not connected.
online	Connected.
op	Attribute the status of IRC channel operator to a user (IRC).
operator	Privileged user of an IRC channel whose role is to inform, help and protect the other users of the channel. The nickname of operators is preceded by an @ sign.
opping	Attribution of the status of IRC channel operator to a user.
over-taker	See *take-over*.
PING	Packet InterNet Groper. Sends a small packet of data to a computer and calculates the response time of this computer.
POP3	Post Office Protocol (version 3). The mail server which receives e-mail to deposit in your mailbox while waiting for you to recover them.
posted message	Message sent between two subscribers without going through their mailboxes (ICQ).
robot	Or bot for short. Program installed in a channel that behaves like a human. It makes it possible to protect the channel and if necessary to attack users and channels. Only the official robots (W or X) are authorised on the Undernet.
script	Automatic procedure for the grouped dispatch of commands and text to a user.
server	Computer providing different services in a network (directory, connection, etc.).
shitlist	List of users that a bot will expel automatically from the IRC channel where it reigns.
smiley	Symbol used to show emotion. For example: :-) means "I am happy."
SMTP	Simple Mail Transfer Protocol. The mail server that handles the mail you send.
spam	Unsolicited message often sent to a large number of persons. These are often advertising or commercial messages.
split	Break of connection between two IRC servers caused by overload. During a split, all the users seem to leave IRC abruptly. They come back a little bit later having the impression that it is the others who split.

take-over	Take over of an IRC channel; an act of piracy. Over-takers temporarily assume the status of operator.
topic	Description of the channel. Only the operators can change the topic.
UIN	See *Universal Internet Number*.
UnderNet	The most popular of the four European IRC networks.
Universal Internet Number	Subscriber number provided by ICQ.
URL	Unique Resource Locator. Universal address of documents on the Web. **http://www.marabout.com**, **mailto:jip@ping.be**, **ftp://ftp.microsoft.com** are URLs.
user@host	Identification of IRC users, composed of the nickname and its IP address. For example: **phil@uk.net**
userlist	List of the nicknames of users present in an IRC channel. This list is updated in real time.
W	In the IRC Undernet network, a robot provided by CService and configured by the operators.
wallop	Messages exchanged by IRC operators (IRCop).
warscript	Hostile script, used in particular during take-overs (IRC).
webCam	Small camera sufficient for the transmission of images via the Internet.
X	In the IRC Undernet network, a robot provided by CService and configured by the operators.

Index